SEIZING
the
TEACHABLE
MOMENT

ALSO BY DR. SHERRY L. MEINBERG

Coping with Urologic Cancers:
A Simple, No Nonsense Guide for Patients

Seizing the Teachable Moment

The Cockroach Invasion

Breadcrumbs for Beginners: Following the Writing Trail

Diabetes ABC

Imperfect Weddings are Best

Recess is Over! No Nonsense Strategies and Tips
for Student Teachers and New Teachers

It's All Thought! The Science, Psychology, and
Spirituality of Happiness (Teacher's Guide)

Autism ABC

The Bogeyman: Stalking and its Aftermath
(TV Premier Episode, Investigation Discovery, 12/12/12)

Toxic Attention: Keeping Safe from
Stalkers, Abusers, and Intruders

Be the Boss of Your Brain! Take Control of Your Life

Chicken Soup for the Kid's Soul (Story)

Into the Hornet's Nest: An Incredible Look
at Life in an Inner City School

SEIZING
the
TEACHABLE
MOMENT

DR. SHERRY L. MEINBERG

authorHOUSE®

AuthorHouse™
1663 Liberty Drive
Bloomington, IN 47403
www.authorhouse.com
Phone: 1 (800) 839-8640

Published by AuthorHouse   05/04/2015

ISBN: 978-1-5049-0751-4 (sc)
ISBN: 978-1-5049-0856-6 (e)

Print information available on the last page.

DEDICATION

This book is joyously dedicated to you, the reader: May this offering of others' experiences help you to see the constant give-and-take, back-and-forth, good-natured exchange of ideas and Teachable Moments throughout your days. We are all teachers, and we are all students. We teach something to, and learn something from, everyone we know—regardless of age. It is good to keep in mind that in order to grow and evolve, we must remain good learners.

CONTENTS

Section Three: LENGTHY LEARNING EXPERIENCES

INTRODUCTION

The teachable moment can happen to anyone (child, student, adult, senior citizen), anywhere (home, school, work, and play), at any time (morning, noon, night), when an interest is piqued by an unexpected observation, question, or world event. Everyone and everything has something to teach even the most accomplished of experts.

The teachable moment is any *unplanned, out-of-the-blue, off-the-cuff* comment, question, or event, that can be used as a learning opportunity. It is a spontaneous response that addresses whatever sparked the enthusiastic interest of an individual or group. It is a fleeting opportunity to address a sudden interest or burning questions in the here and now, when listeners are most open, engaged, and receptive. These are surprising, unexpected, and meaningful moments, that will provide learning that lasts, not to mention special memories. Later, such anecdotes provide great conversation starters.

Consider the controversy surrounding the New England Patriots, alleging their deflating of footballs, in order to have an advantage in the AFC Championship game. This rule-bending situation is being debated from coast to coast, and border to border. Professional players, aspiring athletes, and fans, as well as coaches and trainers of *all* sports—not to mention schools and universities everywhere—are provided such a teachable moment, to show that winning at all costs is not the way to behave. It just isn't fair.

Even Anthony Watts, Baltimore Police Commissioner, said in a recent television briefing (4/27/15), that people should use the Watts, Ferguson, and Baltimore riots as "teachable moments," regarding the senseless lawlessness of looting, trashing property, and setting fire to cars and buildings. Such violence will impact those communities for decades.

Some politicians, as well as business and religious leaders, are often caught with their cheating, or extra-marital affairs, while some movie, TV, and sports stars are often seen exhibiting illegal or bad behavior—all of which make deep impressions on the minds of our youth. These types of situations all provide various don't-even-think-of-doing-this teachable moments, and can be powerful influencers.

Sometimes the teachable moment causes only a brief digression from the subject at hand. Other times, the teachable moment can evolve into a lengthy lesson, or a full-blown unit of instruction, a lifelong interest, or a new hobby. They can all be incredible opportunities to share information or guide others. Most teachable moments are unusual, and unlikely to occur again; a time when everyday occurrences can turn into something extraordinary.

I have pulled out a collection of my previously published personal vignettes, dusted them off, and have included them herein, alongside a smorgasbord of Teachable Moment examples that others have generously offered. Such anecdotes can be helpful and impactful. We learn from others' mistakes and triumphs. And vise versa.

BRIEF LEARNING EXPERIENCES

There are times when a short conversation with an individual—who is in a receptive mood—can make all the difference in an attitude or understanding. Especially, if it is of the don't-even-think-of-doing-this variety. There is a personal engagement with an issue. The response may not always be what you are expecting, however.

RESPECT

When first introduced to the much older principal, one young student teacher responded with, "Oh, you're just the *cutest* thing!" The principal, needless to say, was *not* amused. And his first lecture to her was about manners. Ouch!

Dr. Sherry L. Meinberg

GIVE AND TAKE

I relish the company of people who have done stuff; people who have a knack for creating chaos, walking into drama, or seeing absurdities all around them. Through the masterful storytelling of others, I've learned not to get drunk and pick a fight with guys named T-bone. Or to entertain the flirtations of any woman left at the bar at 2 a.m. and end up getting your motorcycle seat slashed. Also, it's wise to ask what pill that is before you take it from a friend and pop it into your mouth.

Hopefully, I've given back as much as I've received. Maybe my anecdotes have helped young men to understand it's not OK to start a brawl at Norm's Restaurant or flee on foot from San Bernardino cops. But it's fine to run for your life when you brought fists to a gunfight. Live another day, friend.

And tell the story.

Contributed by: Reprinted with permission, from Josh Dulaney, a staff writer for the *Press-Telegram*, Saturday edition (1/24/15) A3.

GOOD INTENTIONS

I was concerned about Hallelujah, one of my best third graders, that year. He was clearly upset. Several times during the hour he came up to me, to whisper his grief about his pet bird that had died that morning. Thinking to console him, I rummaged through stacks of my personal books, and finally found *The Tenth Good Thing About Barney*, by Judith Viorst. The book is about a little boy whose cat had died. I thought it might help Hallelujah to see how another youngster had handled a similar loss.

Later in the day, after I had presented a lesson about continents, and everyone was engrossed in the map follow-up assignment, Hallelujah came up to me, and slammed the book down on my desk. "Well, I read it, but I didn't like it!" he announced.

"But, *why*?" I asked, thoroughly shaken, while mentally flogging myself for my good intentions.

"Because it was sad, and it's too much like what happened to me," he explained. "You know, Ms. Meinberg," he continued softly, "everyone has been so *nice* to me today. And everyone has tried so hard to cheer me up. But you know, I just can't be happy today, no matter what. *It's just too soon!*"

I marveled at the wisdom of this child. I don't like to recall how many years it took me to discover that time, does indeed, heal all wounds.

Point Of View

When presenting the homework assignment to my senior citizens, I was trying to describe the villains they had known. "You know, the potato bugs in your lives."

"Eeeyu!" was the overwhelming response, as they grimaced, and talked over one another. They all had a story.

One woman, however, took another view, entirely. She found potato bugs to be fascinating. We all shuddered and groaned. But she adamantly stood her ground, to the point that I went directly home, and researched them. At length. I still find potato bugs to be icky ("Satan's fetus," as one country calls them), but it was refreshing seeing them from her viewpoint.

Say What?

In the midst of winter, a friend had a visitor from another country. The foreigner asked me—in all seriousness—"Do you belong to the religion that *kills* trees?" I was astounded. Talk about a different perspective during the Christmas season!

Cheese It!

Years ago, when I was in Utah, my son called me in a panic. "Mom! Hurry home! Dad is buying *plastic* cheese!" (My husband had never heard of processed cheese.)

TOTAL STRANGERS

So, I'm walking down a crowded high school hall in my tennis shoes, when my hand is grasped. I'm thinking it's my husband, as we are happily swinging our arms (as we are wont to do, periodically). We turned to look at each other, and simply stared in shocked surprise, as we both started laughing: clearly a case of mistaken identity. And I said, "Well, it's been nice to know you," as we disengaged, and moved off in separate directions. (I was so pleased that the young teenage boy didn't die of horror, to find that he was holding hands with a great-grandmother!)

First Place

Being first in line is a big deal in primary grades. It's *always* been a big deal! Chili, however, carried it to extremes. He would beat everyone into line, early, stake out his position, and wouldn't leave for love or money. As I opened the hall door, a large suspicious-looking puddle extended across the sidewalk, making its way rapidly onto the playground. Some of the children were looking at him in an odd fashion, while others stared with round, disbelieving eyes. Several finally accused him in shocked and disgusted tones, "Chili *peed* on the sidewalk!"

Chili, accustomed to spontaneous invention, quickly said, "Naw, that's just what I *wanted* you to think." Then he launched into a blow-by-blow account of how he had filled his mouth with water at the drinking fountain, and then had spit it out while standing in line. He pantomimed his actions for all to see, and almost everyone accepted his explanation. A few, however, could not be so easily dissuaded from what they had actually seen, staunchly shaking their heads back and forth. "Uh-uh," they intoned, as they pointed accusing fingers at him. "You peed!"

I resisted the urge to play a round of did-too/did-not, and merely waited for the children to tire of arguing about which version of the story was true, while "Ring Around the Rosy" was the background theme music in my mind. I then informed Chili that I *knew* he was guilty of the crime for three reasons. And, for the students' educational benefit, I ticked them off on my fingers: (1) If he had spit the water out of his mouth, the *pattern* of the liquid would be different; (2) There was *too much* liquid involved to have come out of his small mouth; and, (3) The drinking water fountain is cold, and the liquid we were looking at was *steaming*. (I diplomatically refrained from mentioning the many wet spots clustered around the zipper of his jeans.) I felt like Nancy Drew in disguise. (Not for nothing am I hooked on mystery books: They serve as the twentieth-century version of medieval morality plays. And the good guys get to *win!*) Typically, even with the evidence staring him in the face, so to speak, Chili continued to loudly maintain his innocence.

I informed the office of the incident, and demanded that Chili clean up his own mess. The janitor happily supplied a bucket, some soapy water, and a mop for him to use. For some reason, this incident cured his desire to always be first in line.

I Love My Job

I picked up some new brochures at a local Staples the other day. Some college-aged upstart noticed the brochures and asked, "Is that your business, sir?"

(Sir? SIR! I'm not THAT old, dammit!)

I replied, "Yeah." (I'm known for my mastery of the art of conversation, don' cha know?)

He smiled and asked, "What do you do?"

I looked at him for a moment, debating on my answer. I finally replied, "I'm a medium." College Boy stared at me as if I had just said, "Egjs dssd ogcfkkf tuv wandt." So I translated, "I talk to dead people."

The color in his face faded, along with his smile, as his eyes widened. "Oh . . .," he stammered. "Uh, that's cool." He was slowly backing up at that point.

"Oh, I know," I said. "Your grandmother thinks it's pretty cool, too." If his eyes were any wider he would have been painted on velvet.

"She just died!" he exclaimed.

"Yeah, I know," I quipped, as I flicked a brochure with my index finger.

He was gone before the paper stopped vibrating. God, but I love my job!

<u>Contributed by</u>: Charles A. Fillius, known as America's Extra Large Medium. Psychic, Channel, Author, and Cartoonist. He lives in Long Beach, CA, but often flies to other states for bookstore lectures and/or readings. Contact: charles@extralargemedium.net Face-to-face readings or phone readings are offered: 1-928-274-2687

SHOWING EMPATHY

I was subbing with a first grade class, reading them an account of Helen Keller, who was born deaf and blind. With the help of her teacher, Anne Sullivan, Helen Keller found her humanness, and went on to live an exemplary life. The children and I were in the library—they were seated on the carpet, and I was seated in front of them, reading from a book. I like to be as dramatic as I can in my reading to a class, to make it interesting and entertaining. As I was relating the moment when Helen Keller suddenly understood the meaning of what Anne Sullivan was trying to teach her—after living in darkness and silence and ignorance—I surprised and embarrassed myself by choking up with emotion, getting teary-eyed, and not being able to go on. One of the children said, "Mr. Miklosy, your face is all red!" I tried to plow through, but kept choking up. Somehow, I finally made it to the end of that passage. I made light of it, by joking that they'd remember their crazy substitute teacher, who cried while reading a story.

What makes that experience "teachable" is it shows that teachers are people, too, and can be overcome by positive emotions. It validates that possibility for them, as well—of responding emotionally to a beautiful moment. And it teaches them empathy for others.

<u>Contributed by</u>: Leslie Miklosy, a substitute teacher in North Carolina. Mr. Miklosy was born in Argentina of Hungarian parents. He spent his first ten years in South America, and then moved with his parents to the U.S. He learned English as his third language. He has authored three books regarding his offbeat life reflections: *My Thoughts Prefer Side Streets: Collected Essays and Other Reflections; Which is More Round, the World or Your Tummy?: Offbeat Reflections on Serious Living;* and *Thinkerer: A Thinker Who Tinkers with Words and Ideas.*

Clockwork

Just before lunch, the classroom telephone rang. The office wanted to make sure that Yono got the message that he had to be in the office directly after school—at 3:15—for punishment of some playground offense. This surprised me, because he was always so quiet and dependable in class. He was a very sharp, recent immigrant, who had a much greater grasp of the English language than did many locally born inner city children, although some colloquial expressions and idioms gave him pause. I didn't want Yono to bring further trouble upon himself, so I stressed the words "a quarter after" several times, to make sure that he would make it to the office on time. I made a mental note to remind him again when school let out for the day.

After school was dismissed for the day, there was a knock on my classroom door. I opened it, and there stood Yono. All I could think was: *What are you doing here? You belong in the office!*

He solemnly foisted a quarter into my hand. I gave it back to him. He pressed it back into my hand. I returned it, asking what the money was for. This situation was repeated several times. I was having a terrible time, trying to figure out what was going on in his mind. We were still exploring the delicate issue of semantics, when a sixth grade Vietnamese boy sauntered down the hall. We used him as an interpreter. With Yono's limited language, "a quarter after" meant, to him, that if he gave me a quarter after school, he wouldn't have to take the punishment. *Extortion* he understood, telling time, he didn't. It was all a linguistic mix-up; a classic misunderstanding between races. I'm sure that wars have been started in much the same way.

STRANGER ON THE STREET

An unplanned, out-of-the-blue, event occurred during my Life Cycles class, while I was teaching students to meditate and channel energy that might appear, during that 45 minute session. The lights were very low, and I was softly talking while beating my drum, in order to place them in a relaxed state.

The teachable moment was actually directed towards me, the teacher! Approximately 30 minutes into the journey, I opened my eyes to check everyone's energy level, and lo and behold, I looked over and saw the shadow of a man, standing at the registration table! I couldn't see his face, and did not recognize his energy, but realized that he was looking at me, and showing something in his hand. Keep in mind, there was almost total darkness. He was wearing a knitted cap and a ski jacket. I nodded my head for some reason, as an affirmation of understanding him, and he turned around and walked out the door.

Afterwards, I drew the group's energy back to a grounding position, and waited until they were present, in their bodies and their minds. Angie, one of my students, said she saw the shadow of a man in the room, and he was standing behind her with something in his hand. When it was time to raise the lights, we all saw a set of keys on a key ring, laying on the table. It appears that someone had left the back door keys in the keyhole on the outside of the door. So this stranger had walked inside to the front of the building, and entered our dark room—while I was drumming and whispering—in order to return the keys!

This unusual event was a strong teaching moment to myself regarding trust. I just knew we were all safe, and therefore, I remained calm. Afterwards, I realized the strength in all of us, during that mysterious moment, which lasted about two minutes. Stay *strong*, and use your Intuition to handle the Extraordinary.

Contributed by: Jeanie MacDonald, a gifted psychic. She provides seminars and classes (money, intuition, grief, manifesting, etc.) at various sites, and individual readings (half-hour or hour) in her home, or over the phone, or via Skype. Jeanie has an extremely large, devoted following (2,700, at last count). Check out her website: jeaniemacdonald.com

Generation Gap

I recognize that I am a prude, and I do try to combat that trait whenever possible. But, after all these years, I still have trouble talking about specific body parts, and maintain that there are certain things that should remain unsaid, while one is eating.

One night, my husband and I went to dinner at a local restaurant. As the sixteen-year-old hostess was seating us, she loudly exclaimed, "You guys smell just like baby butts!"

Say what! "I beg your pardon?" I strangled in reply, as diners turned to gawk.

"You guys smell just like baby butts," she happily reiterated, as my husband and I exchanged shocked looks and raised eyebrows,

Hmmmm. "You mean like talcum . . .?" I tentively asked, treading lightly, although fearing the worst.

She quickly interjected, "No, no! It's not a *bad* thing. You know, like after a baby's bath, you sprinkle baby powder."

Ahhh, it finally became clear: Baby powder she understood, talcum powder she didn't. It all boiled down to a simple generation gap. Just another linguistic confusion.

SUCCESS!

I'm sitting behind the most autistic boy in a class of autistic children. Seated in chairs in a semicircle and taking turns, they're being led by the teacher in a game that involves social interaction, culminating in throwing a foam ball back to her. I'm substituting for her teacher assistant, who is absent today. Each time it is the boy's turn, I prompt him to throw the ball, but he hasn't been responding. Then, on his third turn, he unexpectedly does throw the ball back to the teacher, and we all—teacher, other autistic students, and I—yell out in unison, cheering his success. It is a sweet moment.

Contributed by: Reprinted with permission from Leslie Miklosy, in his third book, *Thinkerer: A Thinker Who Tinkers with Words and Ideas.* He is a substitute teacher in North Carolina. Mr. Miklosy was born in Argentina of Hungarian parents. He spent his first ten years in South America, and then moved with his parents to the U.S. He learned English as his third language. He has authored two other books regarding his offbeat life reflections: *My Thoughts Prefer Side Streets: Collected Essays and Other Reflections,* and *Which is More Round, the World or Your Tummy?*

DIARY

My eight-year-old daughter, Maliha, was reading the second Harry Potter book, *The Chamber of Secrets*. It features a diary which responds to one of the characters, when she writes her personal thoughts in it. As the story progresses, the diary becomes more sinister and controlling, and ultimately it is revealed that it is controlled by the villain of the series. As we were reading the story, my daughter said, "That is SO SCARY! You think the diary is your friend, but it isn't!"

Seizing the moment, I replied, "That's why we are always talking to you about being safe on the Internet. You might meet someone who says he or she is an eight-year-old, who is interested in the same things that you are. . ."

"But it could be VOLDEMORT!!!"

"Exactly."

[Engaging with others through discussions of books, movies, plays or television, can bring awareness to issues, ignite creativity, or provide understanding, vision, and inspiration.]

<u>Contributed by</u>: Melinda Wells, a Canadian consultant with 15 years of experience in the humanitarian and international development fields. She has worked with the Red Cross, the UN, and NGOs. She is currently a board member for the Collateral Repair Project, a registered 501(c)(3) nonprofit organization; a grassroots effort to bring much needed assistance to refugees and other victims of war and conflict.

Movie Plot

Having spent most of my adult life in law enforcement, I have developed a real interest in our Constitution, and how it affects our daily lives. Recently, my wife and I were watching a movie on TV, in which the plot takes place in Syria. The lead character had fled Syria, and had been tried in absentia and sentenced to death. This was a great opportunity to talk about our constitutional guarantee of a public trial, where the accused must be present, and has the right to confront his accusers. Trials in absentia in America would be unconstitutional. So I paused the movie, and we discussed this constitutional right that we take for granted, until we see how people in some other countries don't have such protections.

Contributed by: Richard Bonneau

CURRENT EVENTS

The events in Ferguson, and other such current events, offered several "teachable moments" about our right to "peacefully" assemble. One event (the convening of the Grand Jury) provided an opportunity to explain that under our Constitution, people may be brought to trial *only* after it has been determined—by either a Grand Jury or at a preliminary hearing—that probable cause exists to believe they have committed a crime. This led to a discussion of the constitutional limitation on the police of arresting someone only when probable cause exists to believe they committed a crime.

Contributed by: Richard Bonneau, after spending 12 years in the aerospace industry, he moved over to the Los Angeles Police Department. He is now a retired captain, after a 37 year career. He was assigned to seven patrol divisions, and worked a variety of assignments, including: vice enforcement, canine operations, Internal Affairs Division, and police academy instructor. As a captain, he commanded the Harbor Patrol Division, and the Scientific Investigation Division, which included the department's crime lab.

SHHHH!

I was scheduled to give a presentation to a school district in Colorado. I flew into the Salt Lake City International Airport, in Utah, through a heavy, driving rainstorm. I was met by two principals, who would drive me to their destination. As we were total strangers, killing several hours, we talked to while away the time. Late in the conversations, grasping for subject matter, one man said, "Oh, I hear that you received your doctorate at BYU." When I answered in the affirmative, he said that he also graduated from BYU, and started quizzing me as to who I knew on campus, name by name. No, no, and no, I responded (after all, it had been several years since I had been on campus). Then he started asking about various professors. Only a few names were familiar to me. Then, seemingly as an afterthought, he asked about one in particular, which I knew well, as he was a professor of a required class for my doctoral group.

Even though we students were all longtime educators and administrators, we raced to the back row in his classroom. The room was small, and closed in, with no air conditioning, and our instructor could sweat, BIG TIME! In addition, he had terrible body odor. Every time he'd raise his arms, the front rows would be practically wiped out.

Deodorant versus antiperspirant became *the* topic of discussion at night, regardless of what we were supposed to be studying. What we learned from that class had little to do with the subject at hand: deodorant keeps you from smelling bad when you perspire, whereas antiperspirant attempts to keep you from perspiring at all. We covered the pros and cons, facts and myths, commercial versus natural deodorant, dry-cleaning problems, and whatnot. "At least the class wasn't a total loss!" I said with a flourish.

An uncomfortable silence inserted itself, before he announced, "He's my brother-in-law."

Good grief! Here I was, in a car with two total strangers, in a different state, and out of millions of people in California, Colorado, and Utah, I have to tell my tale to him. What are the odds? Boy, was my face red. *I determined to never gossip again!* Later, after I twisted in the wind for a while, he admitted that his whole family felt the same way about the professor. But the damage was done.

Hoover Vacuum

My dad worked for Mr. Hoover, as a door-to-door salesman. He once sold a vacuum to a lady without electricity. He explained that it wouldn't work, to which she answered, "I want to be ready!"

(My mom rewound the motors in our kitchen, and one of the vacuums worked for over fifty years.)

[Note: Questions and answers often arise as a result of an unexpected conversation. This type of off-the-cuff comment triggers discussions regarding observations, such as: product quality seems to have declined over the decades. Materials seem less durable, and skilled labor less painstaking; second rate—shoddy, sloppy, or fraudulent—in many cases. *Where is the pride?* Interaction is guaranteed. And you can find who the best electricians, plumbers, painters, gardeners, and so forth, are in your vicinity—as well as which ones to avoid.]

Contributed by: Barbara Kaye Cooper, professional photographer, and computer guru in Long Beach, CA. Contact via: Barbsphoto@mac.com or (562) 420-7508

2ND POSITION EN L'AIR

As a professional dancer, I decided to teach my high school dance class the different positions in ballet. The class was on the stage, and I was on the floor demonstrating 2nd position in the air (en l'air). As I was standing on my left foot, with my right leg out to the side above my waist, and explaining the correct position of the hips, I became aware that the class was mumbling fairly loudly to each other. Without breaking my stance, I asked what was going on. They pointed to my right leg, and said, "You're leg is above your waist, and you're just standing there. How can you do that?"

I brought my leg down, casually raised it back up to the side above my waist, held it there and said, "It takes practice!"

That was it! On their own, they got into pairs and groups, and proceeded to lift each other's leg (right or left) in the air, and try to hold it by themselves. They had more fun, and learned what muscles had to be worked. It was a great impromptu class.

Contributed by: Sally Thompson, retired high school teacher, professional dancer, and university professor.

PRATFALL

It was your everyday normal Monday routine . . . me, the Mom, in my weekly madness of grocery shopping and picking up my two sons from school. This particular spring day, my always jovial, smiling, oldest son, a junior in high school, and on the track team, was unusually quiet and mopey. He hadn't yet even gone through the terrible twos, so of course, I thought today was the day. My youngest son, lagging behind as usual, seemed a bit chipper, which was extremely abnormal for his character. In a moments flash, my maternal instincts kicked in, as the writing was on the wall. My first born child had experienced his first "bad day," and my second son was relishing the fact. Especially since a bad day was a common experience for my freshman. Still, the question was lurking in my heart: "What happened?" Of course, when I asked the question, I received the typical teenage response, "Nothin'!"

I refused to start the car, as I looked in the rearview mirror, and saw my six foot lean machine track star, with his face buried in his hands, softly crying. There was dead silence in the car. At length, the story started to unfold, by my first time ever, devastated, greatest-personality-on-campus, guy. At cross country practice that afternoon, It seems that he had slipped off a curb as they were getting ready to trail run, and went flying to the ground. My son cleared his throat, and tried to act tough, and said that he could handle the scrapes, but the most difficult, embarrassing thing, was that Emilio—the captain of the team, the best-looking guy in the whole high school, the guy who always had the best times in all the meets— THAT guy, teased him uncontrollably. And, to make matters worse, he made these comments in front of all the girls on the girls track team. The Seizing the Teachable Moment came forth, when I simply asked my son one profound question: "Did all the girls come to your rescue?"

And he lifted his head and answered with a big, loud, "YES!" It was at that moment that I made the statement that he so desperately needed to hear: "Emilio was *jealous!*" I declared, explaining that my son had received the attention from an entire squad of females, and it made Emilio—a very, what seemed to be secure individual— insecure and uncomfortable, as all the attention was not on him.

Both of my sons wanted to know how I had detected Emilio's motivation, and my answer was that in life, you learn to never judge a book by its cover. Weeks later, I noticed the top corner of the huge box of laundry detergent that I had purchased that day, that was still in the back seat. Scratched in ink, was the phrase: I "heart" Mom.

Contributed by: Mary Beth Bastio, mother, happy new grandmother, and professional hairdresser.

Disabled?

I was a Senior Instructional Aide for the handicapped students at Warren High School, in Paramount, California. One of the students was a girl who was born without arms from her elbows down, and no legs from her knees down. That was her only handicap, because she was very bright. One day she came into the room during lunch, to have me open a small mustard pack for her sandwich. "No problem," I said. I took the pack, and tried to open it, but my fingers just could not get that pack open. I tried, and tried, to no avail. The girl finally said, "Here, let me do it." She took the pack in her teeth, sat it on her shoulder, and somehow she ripped that pack open.

That was a very teachable moment for me, to see someone who had such a debilitating handicap do something that I, who was not handicapped, could not do. My only regret was that the rest of the class was not there to see that. Many of us complain about small things . . . yet small things can be done.

<u>Contributed by</u>: Corrie Terry, who spent 15 years at Warren High School, in Paramount, CA, as a Senior Instructional Aide for SMH (severely mentally handicapped), with her LVN (licensed vocational nurse) training. She retired when she and her husband moved to Placerville, in Northern California. They have since moved back to Bellflower, in Southern California.

UNANTICIPATED RESULT

"That little bug isn't going to hurt you!" I announced in my most judgmental voice, as the third grade students were quickly shifting positions to get out of its way. We had been sitting in a circle on the rug, quietly reading our textbooks, when a beautiful, iridescent, emerald-green beetle (the likes of which I have never seen, before or since), arrived out of nowhere to interrupt our lesson, and caused every student to disengage. It irritated me that a little insect, the size and shape of a ladybug could command so much attention, even if it *did* move in such a speedy fashion.

No sooner had I made this unfounded statement than the bug circled around and made a beeline right for me. It leaped upon my ankle, and bit me before I could even attempt to move—CRUNCH!—and the pain came in Technicolor.

Immediately, my ankle and foot swelled to such unbelievable proportions that it became difficult to pry off my shoe. The infected area was beet-red, extremely hot to the touch, and started to throb with a rhythm roughly approximating the rate and intensity of a jungle drum. After school, I hobbled over—with one shoe on, and one shoe off—to see the nurse, who gave me a list of addresses of specific district-sanctioned doctors to see on my way home. (Naturally, one doctor was on vacation, and another—situated clear across town in the opposite direction—had moved.) It took me quite a while to find a doctor that was on the list, and, because I didn't have an appointment, I had to wait for a good length of time to see him.

Suffice it to say that I was out of commission for three days, taking anti-venom shots and swallowing anti-inflammatory pills. As a result, this experience taught the students NOT to believe everything a teacher says, and I learned to keep my mouth closed about things I know nothing about. Needless to say, this was a very painful lesson for me to learn, both figuratively and literally.

CAREER CHANGE

From the age of five, I was certain. I knew I would be a doctor. After high school graduation, I attended Boston University as a chemistry major with basic research in biochemistry. As a pre-med student at Georgetown University and McGill University (in Montreal), I was utterly unsure about what kind of doctor I wanted to be. I was pretty sure that I didn't want to be a surgeon. I was equally sure that I *didn't* want to be involved with cancer, as it was distinctly unappealing (few patients improved, and everyone suffered the side effects of chemotherapy).

When I found myself as a first-year medical student seeking basic research opportunities, I first visited with a biochemist. I decided to look elsewhere, and another doctor suggested that I should work with a Dr. Philip S. Schein (who had just arrived at Georgetown from the National Cancer Institute).

Dr. Schein asked what I was interested in, and I told him biochemistry. He said that his lab was studying new forms of chemotherapy. They were synthesizing collections of compounds, and he was testing them on pancreatic cancer. He showed me a chemical structure, and pointed out one of his newest compounds: "an amide." I examined the structure, and then pointed out that it was, in fact, "an imide." He peered back at me, a bit startled, smiled, and said, "You're right . . . Would you like a job?"

"Okay," I replied.

<u>Contributed by</u>: Robert A. Nagourney, M.D., a practicing hematologist/ oncologist. Reprinted with permission from his book, *Outliving Cancer: The Better, Smarter Way to Treat Your Cancer.* (Basic Health Publications, 2013, pp. 7-8). In this book, he shows how he developed a more effective way to treat cancer patients. He has authored over 100 manuscripts, abstracts, and book chapters. In addition, he is a clinical professor—teaching pharmacology—at the University of California, Irvine, as well as the Founder and lab Director at Rational Therapeutics, Inc., a cancer research institute, serving patients worldwide at 750 E. 29th Street, Long Beach, CA., 90806. Contact: (562) 989-6455.

SLIPPING GLIMPSERS

I teach art, kindergarten through eighth grade. When my students reach middle grade, they expect more will be required of them. But in art? No way! I remember one of my sixth graders groaning, "Art's supposed to be fun, not hard!" followed by a chorus of similar protests.

Good grief, I thought. *You're middle schoolers now. Quit your belly-aching!*

A lecture on growing up was about to begin, when I remembered a poem by the artist Willem de Kooning, where he considered himself a "slipping glimpser" all throughout his life. So I blurted out, "You guys are all a bunch of slipping glimpsers!"

They responded with eyeballs connecting sideways with each other. So I wrote it on the board: S-L-I-P-P-I-N-G G-L-I-M-P-S-E-R-S! Then I turned back to them, and asked, "Does anyone remember what it was like, when you first learned to ride a bike?"

"I fell on my butt!" Laughter.

"I was scared."

"I couldn't keep my balance."

I gave them a skeptical look. "Really? You couldn't keep your balance? Why?"

Duh, like because they had never done it before. Next question, teacher.

I pointed to the word 'Slipping' on the board. "You were slipping. Off-balance. It felt hard because it was new." A few nods.

"Why not give up?" I asked.

"I really wanted to ride a bike."

"It got easier."

"Yeah, you're not going to stop when you are getting so close."

I asked, "Close? Close to what?"

"To riding the bike."

"So even when you are really off-balance and slipping, you are telling me that you could see yourself close to actually riding the bike?" I turned toward the board. "What's the word that means you see something, even if it's just for a moment?"

"Glimpser!"

"So, every time you got on that bike, you would glimpse yourself. . ."

"Really riding the bike."

"I would think this time I'm not falling off, I'm staying up. . ."

"So what were you really seeing?"

The kids fell silent, not sure what more I wanted.

I continued, "Here you are, trying something new. It's hard. You are slipping, making mistakes, not feeling so good at it. But you don't give up, because each time you try, you catch a glimpse . . . of what, really?"

One boy spoke up. "That I can do it!"

We continued the conversation about how learning new things can be hard, even in art class. But in taking on fresh challenges, we were really giving ourselves the opportunity to slip into that glimpse of our marvelous potential to achieve something new.

What I didn't tell them? No matter how old we get, we never quit being Slipping Glimpsers.

<u>Contributed by</u>: Elizabeth Call, art teacher at Horace Mann School (K-8) in Hollywoood, CA.

KARMA

When the economy went south in America, I was in a low period of my life, like almost everyone else in the country. Construction jobs were nonexistent (I was standing in the same lines, looking for work, alongside my old bosses), and I was feeling the crunch. I had just bought my dinner at Taco Bell, and had one dollar bill left to my name. I clutched it tightly in my hand, wondering where my next meal was coming from, as I walked out the door and across the parking lot. An elderly man stopped me, asking if I had some change to spare. He looked like he was on his last legs, which gave me pause. There I was, holding my last dollar, and debating the situation in my mind. I was mumbling to myself, "Karma better come through for me, Karma better come through," as I handed over the money. The old man's eyes lit up, as he offered his thanks, and said, as he shuffled off, "I sure hope that Karma gal comes to see you!"

I got a lot of mileage and a lot of laughs from that experience.

[Often the best lessons are learned in the spur of the moment, in the confines of inconvenience and discomfort. Even in the worst of times, funny situations can bring you joy, and lighten your heart.]

Contributed by: Jay Matson, Fresno, CA.

Silence Is Golden

Several years ago, I was having lunch with some teachers at a school where I was a substitute teacher for the day. They were talking about the bilingual Spanish program their students were in. To summarize, it was a program where foreign elementary students would have a daily lesson in English, and then have all their other subjects taught in Spanish, until they reached a certain proficiency level in English. Then they would be taught all other subjects in English, as well.

Along came another teacher to join us for lunch. She said she did not believe students should be speaking any Spanish in class. She said when she was growing up, only English was used, and she learned it very well, thank you. The other teachers at the table remained silent. She continued to go on in her emotionally high strung voice about her objection to Spanish being used, and lessons being taught in Spanish, in an "American" elementary school classroom. I noticed other teachers at the table continued to be silent. Not a word was spoken, neither agreeing nor disagreeing with her. Their silence seemed to speak louder than what any words they could say.

After a while, her voice gradually became calmer, and her tone and words slowly began to change, as she continued to talk while others remained silent. She started to say something like, "Well, maybe it is different for some students at different intellectual levels, and I *was* from a different country. Maybe that makes a difference." The other teachers continued to remain silent. Finally, she said something lime, "Maybe I should look into the matter more, or give it some thought, or maybe some student will benefit more than I did, without using my native language." The change in attitude that she gradually seemed to show broke the ice. The teachers finally all continued a friendly discussion together. The power of silence made a difference.

Contributed by: D.L. Laux. As teacher and a freelance writer, she has worked in elementary schools as a substitute and a 2nd-5th grade teacher, a resource specialist, and a reading specialist. She has written articles for a syndicated newspaper service: "Helping Students Make the Grade," and "Christmas Customs of Other Countries." For the *Instructor* magazine, she wrote, "Whiz Quiz," regarding a learning game where students have fun learning various skills.

BEING A GOOD LISTENER

Are we all buzzing around on send-mode, but rarely on receive-mode? My forty-four year-old son taught me this distinction. One time, when he was upset about something, and was telling me about it, I immediately segued into my problem solving role. He became irritated and defensive. "Mom, I don't need you to fix it. I just want you to listen."

I'm definitely a problem solver—the "fix-it" type. Are you that type? Do you find that when you're just trying to help someone with your sage advice, worldly wisdom, or unsolicited opinion, they become defensive and suddenly dump all their anger on you? Maybe they don't want your advice, wisdom, or opinion. Maybe they just need to rant.

Learning to be a good listener is an art. That's why counselors, therapists, life-coaches, etc., get the big bucks. They have mastered the art of listening with an occasional "oh," or "uh-huh," or "I see."

Occasionally, we all need a sounding board. There isn't necessarily a solution to what we're upset about. We just want to verbalize it. Somehow, doing so to the wall or a chair just doesn't cut it. Why an inert human being hearing our angry commentary seems so comforting is a mystery. Maybe it just makes us feel valid that another sentient being, preferably a human one, cares enough to spend time with us and just listen.

Now, when my son discusses something that is bothering him, and I slip into my fix-it mode, I try hard to remember to ask, "Do you want my input, or do you just want me to be a good listener?" I don't always catch myself, and am still a work-in-progress, but when I do, it has avoided so many arguments, misunderstandings, and hurt feelings. I show that I'm being supportive, that I respect him for being able to handle it himself, and that I'm not being intrusive.

Try it, even if you have to put a piece of tape over your mouth, while doing so. It may save a lot of friction in your relationships.

Contributed by: Lee Gale Gruen. Reprinted with permission from her *Reinventing Myself in My Senior Years* blog of 2/5/15 (LeeGaleGruen.wordpress.com). She retired after a 37-year career as a probation officer, and later became an actress, appearing in TV, commercials, films, theater, and print jobs. Her memoir, *Adventures with Dad: A Father and Daughter's Journey Through a Senior Acting Class* (2013) is available on Amazon (website: AdventureWithDadTheBook.com). Her blog and lectures are aimed at helping seniors find joy, excitement, and satisfaction in their retirement.

Election Day

My husband and I were standing in line before the polls opened, waiting to vote. The workers weren't ready, and the people in line were getting anxious. Some were going to be late for work, and others were going to be late for school. People were grumbling left and right, checking their watches, while huffing and puffing and agonizing.

A man, and his young son (about ten years old) were quietly standing behind us. The man's hands were laced tightly together, as if imposing external restraint. At length, the boy turned to his father, and asked, "Dad, are you mad at me or something?"

The man slightly smiled, and said, "No, son, I'm trying to exercise patience."

His simple demonstration sure helped all those within earshot. Including me.

PSYCHIC

During the first week of the high school year, I gave the students time to get their activity/physical education clothes. Once I declared a due date, everyone was expected to arrive in class, dressed appropriately. Otherwise, they would have to sit outside the building at a picnic table, where they could not watch the rest of the class. This prevented students being stared at by the "nonsuits," thus avoiding others to want to sit and watch the class, as well. Isolation worked wonders!

On the day that the students were to be properly dressed, three girls had neglected to bring their clothes. So, off to the picnic table, outside the gym door, they went. Not, however, without an altercation with one of the girls: Lisa. She was livid! She hadn't been able to get her clothes, because she had slept at someone else's home the night before. Lisa didn't want her gym grade to be penalized because she wasn't dressed, etc., etc., etc. Sorry! Everyone had the same timeframe, everyone had the same rules, and everyone knew the consequences. Outside they went!

A little while later, I decided to check on the three girls. Two were there, but Lisa was gone! Clear across the campus, I saw her by the Snack Area. She saw me, and came racing back all flustered. Not only was she a nonsuit, but she had left the class without permission.

She was very upset, but not for the usual reasons:

"Why had I come out at that particular time, to check on the three of them?

"How had I known to come out and find her gone?"

"How did I know where to look for her?"

"Did I have the Third Eye?"

She bombarded me with these kinds of questions, and seemed somewhat afraid of me.

I simply answered, "I just knew!"

From that point on, I realized that Lisa was convinced that I had the Third Eye. She could not, for the life of her, figure out how I *knew* to come out at that time, and find her gone. I was psychic! I was in full possession of the Third Eye! She also convinced the other students of her feelings.

The fact that it was by pure chance that I chose to check up on the girls at that time, and there was nothing psychic involved, was . . . my secret. So I continued on with my Third Eye. And the class was much easier to manage.

Contributed by: Sally Thompson, retired high school teacher, professional dancer, and university professor.

Happy Hearth Hoo-Hah

My husband and I went to Baja Sonora, in Long Beach, California, for a late lunch. It is a small, extremely popular Mexican restaurant, in which the tables are placed close together, in a friendly, casual atmosphere, to accommodate the crowds. We were quietly eating, when Wayne leaned across the table, and whispered, "I love you."

And a woman at the next table went nuts! "*Did you hear that?*" she announced, in a voice to declare the end of the world. "Did you hear that?" as she pointed at Wayne. "For no reason at all, he just said, 'I love you'—*while they were eating!*" And she continued on in that vein.

Of course, everyone stopped talking and eating, to stare at us. A few voices tentatively called out, asking if we had recently met, or if we were newlyweds. The diners appeared focused and interested. So Wayne felt duty-bound to tell everyone, "No, we've been married for 48 years!" Shock and awe. Then, he continued on, saying, "And we still hold hands." No one could believe it! And he finished, by saying, "And this is the third marriage for both of us!" Which brought down the house. Apparently, we have become an oddity—on many levels.

Experienced at: the award winning Baja Sonora Restaurant, 2940 Clark Avenue, in Long Beach, CA, 90815. (562) 421-5120.

BROKEN TOOTH

Dr. Fishman has been practicing general dentistry for decades, and has always had a fiercely loyal following. A patient called for an emergency appointment for a broken tooth. The secretary told the patient she would see Doctor first, and then she might be referred to a specialist. When the patient arrived, she demanded to know who Dr. First was, and *why* Dr. *Fishman* was not going to see her. It was explained to her that she *was* scheduled to see Dr. Fishman—not a Dr. First.

[Note: Articles of speech are *the* and *a* and *an*, words which express a certain definiteness, usually meaning: one in particular. The most frequent word in the English language is the word *the*. It is most confusing when an article is missing in a sentence:

Remember the sentence that Neil Armstrong famously said, when the Apollo 11 landed? Upon taking his first step on the surface of the moon, he is quoted as saying, "One small step for man, one giant leap for mankind." The missing *a* made a big difference, semantically speaking. Without it, "man" and "mankind" both mean the same thing: all of humanity. It was confusing for a lot of people.

Years later, he explained that no one heard the word *a*. The sentence should have been quoted as: "One small step for *a* man, one giant leap for mankind."]

Contributed by: Bernard Fishman, D.D.S., General Dentistry at 4403 Los Coyotes Diagonal (Outer Traffic Circle), Long Beach, CA. 90815. (562) 425-6611.

Again And Again

Francis enrolled as a third grader late in the school year. She did the work expected of her, and took part in daily activities in a robot-like way—with no emotion involved—but she wouldn't speak. She had not uttered a word to anyone, not even me. She and her beloved sister had recently been separated, taken away from abusive parents, and placed in separate foster homes. Francis was having a hard time adjusting to the loss of her *total* family, as well as a new family, a new neighborhood, a new school, a new teacher, and new classmates.

She followed directions well, making no trouble for anyone, but took part in school activities with all the joy of a wind-up toy. She had definitely been traumatized by her experience. Since we didn't know what would work, we did what we could, feeling our way, by guess and by golly. The class tried new things to interest her every day, hoping to find the combination that would open Francis like a safety-deposit box, to no avail.

Finally, after three weeks, she became one with the group—during music, of all things. I was teaching the class to sing a two-part melody, titled, "White Choral Bells." We were doing a grand job of harmonizing, when her voice joined ours in song. It was immediately apparent to all. I could see the youngsters' bright eyes and smiling faces, as they continued to happily sing. Frances had finally decided to become a full-fledged member of our class family. She later confided, shyly and hesitantly, that her big sister used to sing that song, and it reminded her of the good times they had shared together. We made it a point to sing it often.

A Special New Year's
Eve To Remember

A month after I started chemotherapy, 16 years ago, on the last night of what ha been a very tough year, I sat by the fire in our living room, with my husband, my mother, and my daughter.

Only a few wispy bangs hung on, along with some stray red hairs sticking straight up from the top of my head. Without hair, my ears seemed huge.

"I look like Father Time," I joked.

"You have an elegantly shaped head," George told me—perhaps the most romantic thing anyone ever said to me.

My tummy wasn't much up to Champagne, but Mom brought me warm ginger ale in a crystal goblet, so I could join in the midnight toast. She had come from her home in Virginia to stay with us, and help me through my recovery after breast cancer surgery. What we thought would be a three-week visit extended into several months, when it turned out I needed chemo.

George had surprised us girls with matching red plaid flannel nightgowns that year, which we were all wearing. I remember Mom laughing that the only time in her life she got a gift from Victoria's Secret, it was from her son-in-law!

Sara, just out of grad school and living in her first apartment, came to spend the special night with me. And the four of us—Sara always says George is one of the girls—had a strange and wonderful pajama party. One I will never forget. It forever defined where I want to be on New Year's Eve—in front of a fire, surrounded by love.

Contributed by: Patricia Bunin. Reprinted with permission from her Senior Moments column for the *Press Telegram* newspaper (Sunday edition, 12/28/14, Health section, p.3). Her weekly column appears in six other newspapers. She has authored *Password: SeniorMoments,* a collection of personal vignettes that illustrate how aging adults design and define their lives. (At the starstuck age of 13, she interviewed Elvis Presley, and he played his guitar and sang to her, and then kissed her goodbye. It was her first kiss, and it changed her life forever. She now has a large, framed poster of Elvis that hangs over her desk.)

Paperwork Problems

In the course of performing my work, decades ago, there were errors on the vessel manifest that I was responsible for. I worked at the Port of Long Beach, employed by Intl. Transportation Service, Inc. for 33 and a half years. I was a vessel coordinator, in the Operations Department. In the 80s, I was involved in a very odd situation.

Just before leaving on my two week Christmas vacation, a co-worker was on Jury duty, and, as such, was not required to come in on Saturday. So I covered for her. I arrived at 7:45 A.M. It was supposed to be a short shift, and appeared to be an easy day, so I looked forward to leaving early. Famous last words.

I was dealing with an older, smaller ship, with only 200 containers to be moved (the bigger ships held 4,000 to 6,000 containers each), with a deck limit of 80 feet. Since this ship was older, the hatch covers were rated to hold a maximum of 80 tons. But as most of the full 40' containers weighed close to the maximum rate of 30 tons, we could not load 3x40' on top of each other, as they would have weighed approximately 90 tons (10 tons over the maximum allowed). But those three 40-foot containers needed to be housed together. The longshoremen wanted to fit different containers together, but I had to stop them from doing so, because those boxes would also be over-weight, which would exceed the deck limit.

In addition, specific laws prohibited stacking containers in certain ways. For instance, you can't put empty containers in the hull, and full containers on the deck, as the ship would be top heavy, and prone to turning over. And there were five containers that couldn't be split apart. And although the underdeck stowage didn't have the same weight restrictions, hazardous cargo cannot be placed under the deck, or below the hatch cover, and had to be at least 90 feet—two hatches—away from the wheelhouse, which complicated matters. It was the accumulated weight that was the problem for loading, which was very time consuming.

I had to change the manifest, every time the longshoremen would change the containers in each section. It was the weight limitations that created the revisions. And the computer was taking far too long printing revisions, because each time we made a change, it would rerun *the entire ship's cargo* by load and by weight, in which bays or area of the ship, with each number having corresponding code numbers, plus the yard location (yard container or pallet), instead of just the one section we were working on. So timing became an issue.

At midnight we were still there. The day shift of longshoremen had already left, as they had exceeded their overtime, and the night shift came on board. And since we had to be finished by 3:00 A.M, I started working everything out in handwriting. Finally, my revised official document showed everything on board, with a detailed description of the whole stowage plan. With my paperwork completed, I dragged on home to start my vacation.

This second group of longshoremen weren't happy, being on such a tight schedule. So, saying a mental, "Screw you, lady! We're putting them where we want!", they proceeded to do so, willy nilly. Paying no attention to the manifest, they placed the containers wherever they would fit, in an effort to beat the clock. And were done on time. And the ship set sail on time.

At some point, for no known reason, the ship changed course. It was originally headed for one port, but it had a last minute diversion, and actually landed in Port Lazaro Cardemas. "Where's that?'" Everyone wanted to know. Then, since the unloaded cargo wasn't in the same order as the manifest, the containers were opened. As it turned out, five of the ten containers marked fireworks, were actually full of guns. To complicate matters, the packing slip on the outside of the crates said their destination was England, whereas the inside packing slip said East Germany. *Say what?*

As a result, the ship was detained, with armed Mexican guards patrolling the area. So, many countries got involved in the incident, because all of the guns, as well as all the other cargo, was stolen from the ship. And no one knew how that had happened. More confusion.

Not knowing any of this, I was blissfully enjoying my vacation. I watched Ollie North, getting in his car, on the television, being beseiged by news reporters, yelling constant, "Is it true . . . ?" questions at him, with him responding, "At least you could say, 'Did you have a Merry Christmas?'"

In the meantime, the FBI shows up to ask my employer about me. When he inquired as to why they were interested, he was told, "None of your business. It doesn't concern you." Next came Interpol (U.S.A.), the CIA, and Interpol (Mexico City), and ATF (local), and AFT (Mexico), waiting for me to return from my vacation. My boss told all of the interested parties that I would be back on January 2nd. He was then told that as soon as he saw the whites of my eyes, he was to call them all. *Immediately.*

Now I knew that I had an extra day coming for vacation—since I had worked such long hours on that last day—so I called in on the 2nd, to tell them I would be taking another two days off. Everyone was freaked, as the tension mounted, and imaginations went wild.

When I finally walked into work, my co-workers were snickering and calling me "Jailbird." *Uh-oh, what's that all about?* I was thinking, as my tight-lipped boss emphatically pointed me directly upstairs (which always meant someone was in BIG trouble). And I said, "At least you could have asked if I had a Merry Christmas!" a la Ollie North. No one would tell me what was happening. But then, they really didn't know either.

Then he called all the alphabet letter groups involved. They said not to let me out of the room. So I waited. And waited. And waited. Much later, they gave me a juice break, and I called my mom to pick up my kids from school, as I didn't know how long I would be. At 3:00 my boss was called, and told that the group was waiting for the top man from Interpol, Mexico, who was flying in to talk with me. At 5:00 P.M. I was finally escorted to the conference room.

How intimidating! *Twelve men*, in the finest suits I have ever seen, were waiting for me. They quizzed me for hours, asking the same questions over and over and over again. They were especially interested in why I stopped using the computer, and started working with pen and paper. (Since that experience, the powers-that-be fixed the computers so they no longer crank out the whole shipment, and you can work on one section at a time!) Unfortunately, the men didn't speak English, and had brought their own interpreter (who wore a polo shirt), but his English wasn't even near perfect. So there was a lot of wasted time, trying to figure out exactly what I was saying. Luckily, I had saved all of my paperwork, showing every single change, and I was able to explain what I had done, and why. But no one would tell me what was going on. I thought of stowaways, illicit drugs, human trafficking, and pirates. It was nerve-racking! I never even once considered gun-running.

At length, they had the President of the Scandinavian shipping company, fly in from New York, to be questioned about the procedures of the Port's manifests. Of course, he didn't know. And about six months later, his company went belly-up.

Finally, I was told that it was a "clerical error" having to do with "questionable cargo," as the insurance company for the ship had to pay out one and a half million dollars for the stolen goods.

Which just goes to show that when a comedy of errors is involved, it's better to learn from other's mistakes, than to make them on your own.

Contributed by: Peggy Wright. Retired. Long Beach, CA

WILD, WILD WEST!

When one of my twin daughters, Shari, was only 12 years old, she became fascinated with the Mae West movies she saw on television. She found Mae to be not only entertaining and clever, but also a very underestimated comedienne. She told me wanted to meet Mae, to interview her for the school paper, of which she was the editor. At the time, Mae West was alive and well, and in her 80s.

Most kids who make a request like that would have little hope of accomplishing their desire, but in Shari's case, there was a distinct possibility it could be done. Her father, Irwin Zucker, a Hollywood publicity agent, had the connections to most of the stars in town, and arranged the Mae meeting for Shari.

So it came to be that her request was granted by this legendary actress, but Mae made a request also. There would be no cameras, no tape recordings, and Shari would only be granted 15 minutes for her interview. Shari could take the old reliable pen and notebook, and her old reliable mother to drive her to Mae's penthouse in the apartment building that Mae owned in Hollywood, on Rossmore Avenue.

Well, it turned out to be quite an experience. For starters, Mae and Shari hit it off like old friends. Mae made her grand entrance about five minutes after her butler let us in.

In true Mae West elegance, she glided into the room on white high-heeled pumps supporting her dainty feet, and her white feather-trimmed floor-length satin gown. She still had her long, platinum-colored hair, and was in full make-up. She wasn't about to let a fan see her au naturel, the way so many stars do these days.

In person, Mae was not a big woman, possibly five feet one, but her ample bosom gave her the appearance of being much bigger when she graced the silver screen. Everything in Mae's apartment was like a backdrop for her. White walls, white satin sofa, white satin-finished piano, and even her butler was dressed in white. It was easy to see what her favorite color was.

Mae told Shari stories about making movies in Hollywood's heyday, and how much she disliked W.C. Fields, because he had abandoned his wife and children. It was Mae who was kind enough to send them money, because W.C.'s imbibing of alcohol seemed to leave him without a conscience, or a memory of his family. You could get an idea of his curmudgeon personality by one of his famous quotes: "Start the day with a smile, and get it over with!"

The designated 15 minutes stretched to three hours, with Mae bringing out her scrapbooks depicting her career from the 1920s to the then 1970s, and telling my daughter that she was 28, and if you turn that around, you'd know how old she was! She said a reporter once called her a "gold digger," but she stated, "No gold digging for me, I take diamonds!" Something my daughter took to heart.

After three hours, it was I, the weary mother, who said we had to leave. Then Mae graciously brought out some souvenir gifts for my delighted daughter: a silver bracelet, matching silver belt, and three autographed pictures of Mae. One for Shari's twin, Judi, one for me, and of course, one for Shari.

We were standing in Mae's doorway, saying goodbye and thanking her for such an interesting afternoon, when an earthquake hit, and the whole building began to sway. Up to that moment, Mae had spoken normally, but in a split second, she went into her "Mae West" act, put her hand on her hip, and in her famous on-screen sarcastic wit, she said, "Well, you don't make much of an entrance, but you make one HELL of an exit!"

Of course, she broke the nervous tension, and we all laughed through the next 20 seconds, proving that even at 82, she was still sharp, and funny as ever. Also proving that one of her many famous quotes was also true about her: "It isn't what I do, but how I do it. It isn't what I say, but how I say it—and how I look when I do it and say it!"

We are glad we took to heart another famous quote of hers, and went up to see her sometime. That "sometime" will stay in our memories forever.

Mae believed in the spirit world, telling us she had seen one of her dead relatives sitting on her sofa the week before.

Mae was born on August 17, 1893, and returned to the spirit world November 22, 1980, at the age of 87. We are sure she's got those spirits laughing in the great beyond right now!

Contributed by: Devra Z. Hill, Ph.D. Reprinted with permission from *Chopped Liver for the American Spirit* anthology. She is the author of *Rejuvenate, The Best of Your Life for the Rest of Your Life*, and *What Almost Happened to Hedy Lamarr*. She does radio shows across America about Hollywood and health. She and her publicist husband, Irwin Zucker, have twin daughters (both authors), and five grandchildren. Check out her website: devrazhill.com

LONGER LEARNING EXPERIENCES

The Teachable Moment is often apparent when a significant emotional or traumatic event occurs. The timing is right when, at that precise moment, a unique or high interest situation lends itself to a discussion of a particular subject, leading to meaningful, substantial, and sustainable change.

Unexpected Intrusion

The tenth grade Poly High School student teacher was freaked! She had apparently taken the wooden sign that read: THERE CAN'T BE A CRISIS TODAY; MY SCHEDULE IS ALREADY FULL to heart. Her lesson was in shambles. She had barely begun her presentation, when the door slammed wide open, and six police officers trooped in, with a drug dog. The dog, and its trainer, walked up and down each row, checking out the students and their belongings. Then half of the class went outside to speak with the officers. When they came back inside, the other half went outside, to take their turns. At length, two of the boys were handcuffed, and taken away, never to be seen again. The student teacher was most concerned about not being able to follow her lesson plan. Not to worry: That was the perfect time for a meaningful discussion regarding drugs, as every single student was already focused on the topic. It was a great Life Lesson. Be flexible.

SAFETY FIRST!

All 120 third grade students were seated out on playground, watching a Bus Safety Demonstration. A large school bus was parked on the school blacktop, with the students sitting in an orderly fashion, facing the bus. The bus driver, and a district official, were instructing the students on the proper way to exit through the back of the bus, in case of an accident or emergency situation. The principal then invited a teacher to demonstrate how to follow said directions. She was reluctant to do so (in high heels, and all), but duty called. Unfortunately, as she nervously moved through the back door, she misstepped and fell. The students saw her lose her balance, and watched her undignified plummet. They heard the thud of her body hitting the pavement, and her moaning in agony. Everyone was horrified, and so shocked, no one moved for a moment—it had happened so fast!—and it was hard to wrap their minds around what they had just witnessed. Then a flurry of action took place, as the bus driver ran to get his walky-talky, and summoned an ambulance. Luckily, the fire station was only a few blocks away, and a short time later, an ambulance came screaming onto the playground. Everyone watched as the teacher was placed on a stretcher, quickly moved inside the ambulance, and spirited away to the closest hospital. Of course, when back in their classrooms, the *only* topic of conversation was on the health of the teacher, safety in general, and bus safety in particular. It was later confirmed that the teacher's leg was broken. Everyone was reminded that **safety never takes a holiday**. They learned to be careful, focus, and watch their step!

FIRE DRILLS

I had arrived at Wilson High School for my first observation with a student teacher, to find that the master teacher was absent and a substitute was filling in. I no more than opened the classroom door, when the Fire Bell began ringing. Neither the substitute, the student teacher, nor I, knew where to go. Since this was the start of a new school year, neither did the freshman students. Although we were situated in front of all the other bungalows, we had to wait and follow the last class out. And we still didn't know where to line up, and simply took a space that looked large enough to accommodate us all. The sad part was that the Long Beach Fire Department was out in full force, doing their required evaluation for the school. I'm sure our confusion didn't help matters.

A similar experience happened at Jordan High School. Again, I was observing a brand new student teacher (under recent contract), when the Fire Bell rang. She didn't have a clue as to what to do, or where to go. Since we were on the third floor of the science building, that information was imperative. Luckily for us, it was just a drill.

I just happened to be observing in an elementary school, for two separate fire drills, a year apart. During the second, the kindergartners were led to the sidewalk less than six feet from their classroom. If that wing of the building had been on fire, this would not be a safe place to be. I knew that all the classes were assigned specific places on the playground, at the opposite end of the school, and asked about the situation. It turned out that the master teacher was *tired*, and just didn't want to walk that far. Wrong! In a real emergency, everyone would be looking for that class, thinking the worst. Not to mention, the very real risk involved.

In all of the above examples, the student teachers immediately realized that they must find out where their students were specifically assigned to line up for fire drills, and go there, drill or no drill.

Honesty Is The Best Policy

Years ago, I was shopping with my three children in this pretty little boutique. I felt a headache coming on, and when it came time to pay for my items, I failed to notice that the clerk had undercharged me by about $15.00. It was only after I got home that I noticed the problem with the bill. It was too far to drive all the way back to the boutique, so I quickly added up the prices of the items that had been left off, calculated the sales tax, and then sent a check to the shop with a note explaining what had happened.

Several days later, I received a lovely thank you note in the mail. The people at the shop were simply flabbergasted that I had taken the time and effort to address the discrepancy. They complimented me on my integrity and thanked me profusely, saying I had reaffirmed their faith in mankind. I showed the note to my children, and a teachable moment was born. They were impressed with the letter I had received, even more so since the school theme for that particular year was—you guessed it— integrity. Coincidence? I wonder.

<u>Contributed by</u>: Theresa Schultz, Editor, OC SinC newsletter (Orange County, CA, Sisters-in-Crime national mystery writing organization). She is a freelance writer and editor, who lives in Southern California. She is happy to take on new clients, and can be reached at: theresaschultz@cox.net.

CHARLIE BROWN

One February morning, many years ago, my third graders—who were always so happy and excited about anything and everything in life—were quietly lined up *before* the bell rang. They weren't into playing games that morning, as per usual, and all were seemingly thinking their own thoughts, and not interacting with each other. A gloomy pall had settled over the entire group. *What in the world?!* I thought, as they entered the classroom, without the usual amount of rambunctious energy, smiles, and greetings.

So I chucked the beginning morning exercises, and asked them what was wrong. Very little response was forthcoming. Finally, after some prodding, they explained that Charlie Brown didn't get any valentines. *Say what?* The now classic Valentine Day cartoon TV program had premiered the night before, and the whole class was touched by the story. All of the students showed a caring concern about the situation, and all had a soft spot in their hearts for Charlie Brown. Empathy was strong. Suddenly, as if a dam had broken, they all offered their feelings (sad, angry, disbelief) on the subject.

So, the morning lessons went out the window, as they all wrote heartfelt letters to Charlie Brown (something they *wanted* to do, as opposed to an impersonal assignment). Afterward, they made original valentines, happily coloring, cutting, and pasting. Thereafter, I showed each valentine to the group, as they oohed and ahhed over their classmates' artwork. The pupils watched as I placed them all in a huge envelope, addressed to Charles Schultz. I mailed it that evening on the way home, and promptly forgot about it.

Several weeks thereafter, a large envelope arrived at the school, for Room 21. Within it, we found a long personal letter from Charles Schulz, and a large glossy photograph of the Peanuts Gang with each of their signatures (a nice touch), and a set of coloring pages for each student. Wow! That impromptu lesson was meaningful in many more ways than one.

RISK IS THE BALM

One evening, I eagerly began my first reconnaissance mission back to California, where I would soon be starting my life anew. With a farewell to New Mexico, where I'd been living for the past ten years, I happened to stop at a 7-11 for a grapefruit juice. I was already an hour on the way to LA from Santa Fe, feeling very excited to make my grand appearance in the Golden State, on Valentine's Day of 2010. I imagined that I'd arrive in the easternmost suburbs of LA around 7:00 in the morning, and was not really looking for any detours or distractions along the way.

As I left the 7-11, entered my car, and opened my juice, just before starting the engine, I noticed this amazing gal across the way. And our eyes connected. A moment later, she and her female friend were at my window asking if I could help them, since they'd just been robbed, and had nothing more than the clothes remaining on their backs. Now, usually I would have given a dollar to such transients and addicts, and been on my way. Instead, I welcomed them into my life, and they took me on a three-week adventure of a lifetime. Those three weeks became the subject of my first true novel, *Babie Girls*, that I am now beginning to pitch to the world, in my new home of Los Angeles. I am very happy that I seized this opportunity to learn, to connect, and evolve.

<u>Contributed by</u>: David Beakel, a writer, mountaineer, naturalist, and photographer, now based in Hollywood. He has a degree in physics and biology. Check him out on Facebook.

GROSS!

As I waited for the third graders to straggle into line, the first one crowded so close she ended up on my foot. As usual. *Why is it that students always stand on my feet?* I asked myself for the umpteenth time, as I bit back a shriek of pain. They seem to want to get as close as physically possible. It's no wonder my feet hurt so much when I get home.

While standing on my foot, waiting for the bulk of my class to arrive after recess, the first student looked straight up into my face, and made a shocking discovery. "Ms. Meinberg, Ms. Meinberg! You have *hairs* up your nose!" she announced in a voice that could be heard two blocks away.

Everyone immediately jostled around for a better view. *Oh, Geez, why me?* I silently implored the heavens. "Yes," I smiled. "*Everyone* has nose hairs."

"Say *what*?"

"No way!"

"Not me!"

"Uh-uh!"

The group members yelled in ragged concert, spontaneously clasping their hands over their noses. They were all nodding in agreement: *No one* had nose hairs, but me. I did my best to quickly explain the concept of cilia, but the students weren't buying any of it.

Since nobody admitted to the possession of an inquiring mind, and seeing that I couldn't convince them (it was just TOO GROSS for them to even consider!), I immediately launched into a mini-health lesson about cilia, the purposes for, and so forth. The pupils found various books on the subject, and I dragged out my large nose posters, and we had an impromptu lesson right then and there, comparing and contrasting information from several sources. (My motto is: Strike when the iron is hot! I'm a great one to rearrange the schedule for *meaningful* learning to take place.)

Even with information from several different health, science, and reference books—not to mention pictures and posters galore—no one *wanted* to believe it. So, I lugged out my coffee can full of small mirrors, and passed them out. The children checked out their own reflections, as well as each others. *Wow!* It was like pulling teeth, but they were finally convinced that *everyone* had hair up their noses, whether they liked the idea or not.

The students learned the correct scientific/biological/medical term: cilium (single form), and cilia (plural form). They thought cilia was a silly-sounding word, and enjoyed saying it. The class finally understood that the function of cilia is to trap or catch dust particles (pollen, bacteria, and viruses), to keep them from invading their respiratory system. We drilled each other, orally, on the reasons for cilia, so they could later inform their family and friends of same:

"Hair up your nose is a good thing. Cilia keeps your body safe."

"Dust sticks to nose hairs, called cilia."

"Cilia sweeps away the bad stuff, like a broom."

"Just like eyelashes protect your eyes, cilia protects your insides."

"Cilia keeps all the bad stuff from going into your body."

The third graders couldn't wait to get home, to tell everyone that each and every person actually had such a horrible thing as hair up their noses. There's nothing like a gross out lesson, to get the kids' attention!

How To Be Reckless
In Your Old Age

Many years ago, while living in New York City, I once walked over a hundred blocks late at night, in the dark of Manhattan. I'd finished a heavy meal at an Indian restaurant in the Lower East Side, and had decided, on the spur of the moment, to "walk it off" going back home. Instead of taking the usual subway, I set out on foot around 11:00 P.M., and got to my apartment in the Upper West Side at I:00 A.M.

It wasn't a smart thing to do, and I only did it once. Of course, my recklessness easily could have gone badly—and then I'd be giving this example for a different life lesson, if at all. I recollect it fondly, as a foolish adventure.

We generally should use reason and common sense to guide us, to protect ourselves from the world. And, as we get older, we have even more cause to be careful in what we do. Our stamina, for example, is in shorter supply, there's now a certain brittleness to our mental and physical constitution; our response and recoup times are a fraction of what they were. Let's face it: As dumb as risky choices might have been in our youth, they're downright stupid in the light of accumulated years. Lapses in judgment have no place in the halls of hard-earned maturity.

And yet, we always yearn for a little excitement in our lives, no matter our age. It's the flavoring, if you will, that enlightens the trodden routine of our days. Maybe especially it's true, as we navigate in our so-called golden years more deliberately, more efficiently, and—sadly—more laboriously.

If we decide to choose some modicum of recklessness now and then, know it has adjustable parameters. I'm not suggesting jumping out of airplanes (former president George H.W. Bush's birthday skydiving jumps notwithstanding); or running with the bulls in Pamplona, Spain; or taking up extreme skiing in the European Alps. We need to honor our limits, just as we should honor our zest and adventure. Push gently against the words, "I can't" and "I shouldn't."

Levels of risk—and amounts of risk—require our experience, judgment, and intelligence to evaluate. Even race-car drivers wear seatbelts and helmets. I don't guarantee results, of course, or take responsibility for bad outcomes other than my own. After all, if you want the rewards, you have to own the gamble.

Life can be dressed up, engaged in with all the bells and whistles we can muster, and even celebrated as an extravaganza. There's pleasure to be had, to that last breath we take. If opportunities exist to do what might quicken our breath, or bring a covert and embarrassed smile to our lips, or challenge our sense of humdrum inevitability, why not skillfully grab them?

<u>Contributed by</u>: Leslie Miklosy. Reprinted with permission. Printed in the *Fayetteville Observer* newspaper, Saturday Extra (2/17/15). Leslie Miklosy, is a substitute teacher in North Carolina. He was born in Argentina of Hungarian parents. He spent his first ten years in South America, and then moved with his parents to the U.S. He learned English as his third language. He has authored three books regarding his offbeat life reflections: *My Thoughts Prefer Side Streets: Collected Essays and Other Reflections; Which is More Round, the World or Your Tummy?: Offbeat Reflections on Serious Living; and Thinkerer: A Thinker Who Tinkers with Words and Ideas.*

DIVE BOMBERS

And then there's the time when three summer school classes walked to the El Dorado Nature Center, in Long Beach, California. The students had congregated at the main building to tour the exhibits. Unexpectedly, bees from a nearby hive dive-bombed everyone! In a split second, the air was full of tiny yellow bodies and cries of pain. Children charged off every which way, some with five or six welts each, and others without any, but everyone hysterical, nonetheless. Needless to say, all were preoccupied with bee stings, and little other learning took place that afternoon. It was the perfect time, however, for creative writing, and to introduce Rimsky-Korsakov's "Flight of the Bumblebee" for music appreciation. The following day, the class compared and contrasted said music with that of B. Bumble and the Stingers' "Bumble Boogie." The third graders loved it. Ah, timing!

PERSISTENCE PAYS OFF

Way, way back, when I was a seven-year-old third grader, I loved to play baseball. The big boys (5th, 6th, and 7th graders), always played 500 in front of my house. (It was a noncontact game, in which the batter would hit the ball, and the players would get so many points for catching it: 100 points for a fly ball, 50 points for one bounce, 25 points for a two bouncer, and 10 points for grounders.) I would sit on the curb, watching, aching to take part, and periodically asked if I could play. They always refused, since I was a little girl. Finally, the boys tired of running after some of the grounders in the next block, and let me chase after them. So I would stand behind six or seven guys, and run after the rolling balls that no one wanted to bother with. One day, I actually made 500 points. Then all the boys rushed toward me, begging to take my place at bat. I refused, walking through an angry gauntlet. As I picked up the bat, they all moved up as close as possible. I kept telling them to back up, because I was worried about hitting them, when I swung the bat around. They reluctantly took a couple of steps backward. Satisfied that I had a bigger space in which to swing, I threw the ball up, and when it came down, I socked that sucker clear into the next block! The way their heads followed the arc of the ball, and their whistles, shouts, and wild responses as they chased after it, was very satisfying to me. And I got to play 500 with them forever after. It was the first major achievement of a goal that I was really proud of, but I never told anyone about it. It was personal.

ONE EXPERIMENT TURNS
INTO OTHERS

When I was teaching biology for non-majors at Glendale Community College, I created a simple experiment to teach the students about the scientific method. Each student would get a plastic Petri dish containing agar for growing bacteria. The students would bisect the dish by drawing a line with a grease pencil. Then they would open the dish, and touch one side of the dish, leaving fingerprints on the agar with unwashed hands. Then they would wash their hands with soap, and after drying with a paper towel, they would repeat their actions on the other side of the plate.

After a few days, they would count the number of bacteria colonies on each side of the plate, and determine there were more bacteria that would grow on the dirt vs. the clean side. When the students looked at their plates, they were shocked to see that the dirty side had a number of colonies, but the clean side had hundreds of colonies. I asked them where they thought all the bacteria came from. We repeated the experiment, but this time, half of the class dried their hands with the paper towels, and the other half air dried their hands. When we compared the results, the students who dried with the paper towel had the same result. The students who air dried their hands had very few bacteria on the clean side. We discovered that the paper towels were loaded with bacteria that would grow on the agar dish.

The next experiment was created by the students. One student wanted to compare tap water to bottled water. My initial instance was to say no, that there would be very little, if any, in both types of water. We were both surprised with the results. There were no colonies growing on the tap water side, but the bottled water side had many colonies.

I asked the student how he got the bottled water. He said he got it from a bottled water dispenser. This was an opportunity to carry the experiment one step further. I asked the student to repeat the experiment, but this time, he was to get the water from an unopened five-gallon bottle of water. The results were as expected: very few, if any, bacteria colonies.

The class learned a good lesson, which is, when you pour clean water into a dirty container, the water does not remain clean. When the student took the container apart, he found algae growing in the water dispenser. Periodic cleaning of the water dispenser is just as important as the water you put in it.

Contributed by: Steven R. Kutcher, Biology Instructor, West Los Angeles College. Mr. Kutcher is also a world-famous entomologist and environmentalist. He has presented hundreds of popular insect show-and-tell talks at schools, libraries, museums, fairs, and to interested groups of every kind. His insects are used in movies, television shows, and commercials. Check out his website: Bugs Are My Business. (He even sells art note cards that his insects have painted.) Very interesting.

Up Close And Personal

My two sons, Danny (age 13) and Jay (age 6), and I were fishing from the beach, in the ocean waters of Seal Beach, California, one night. We were fishing for barred perch. The grunion were running at the same time, so many people were walking around with their flashlights, or wading in the surf. Everyone was killing time, simply waiting for the grunion to run. I hooked a leopard shark—a female, over five feet long, and brought her in. It was apparent that she was pregnant, so we treated her gingerly. The boys dug a long trench in the sand, and placed a huge plastic tarp along the bottom, and they filled the trench with buckets of water. Then the three of us carried the shark, and carefully laid her in the long hole.

The boys placed our Coleman lanterns around the area, so people could see how beautiful the shark was, with spots just like a leopard. It was the first time most visitors had ever seen a live shark, and much oohing and ahhing took place. Everyone had many questions about the shark (How big are its teeth? What does it eat? and so forth), which both boys happily answered. They were excited to share what they knew. It was enjoyable to hear their confident replies, and watch their interactions with the public. Although young, they were already seasoned fishermen.

When I was asked: "Where was it caught?" I pointed straight out to the ocean surf, and no one could believe that they were wading in the same foam in which the shark had been swimming. They were further surprised to find that she was also looking for grunion, as were other species of sharks (shovel-nosed and gray sharks), alongside cow-nosed rays, yellow-fin croakers, corbina, and small stingrays, that stayed a little further off shore.

The boys frequently changed the water for the leopard shark. Some of the more adventurous visitors wanted to touch her, and were totally amazed that she felt like sandpaper. People learned a lot from the boys, who were excited to share their knowledge. Later, the three of us delicately lifted the leopard shark, and carried her back into the ocean, where she peacefully swam away.

This impromptu hands-on experience turned two youngsters into unexpected teachers, and visitors of all ages into learners. *How fun is that?!*

Contributed by: Wayne M. Meinberg, retired from Rancho Los Amigos Medical Center, after 30 years of service. He lives in Long Beach, CA.

American Legion Post #134

As the President of the American Legion #134, in Paramount, California—in continued devotion to our fellow service members and veterans—I, along with the women in our group, put together boxes of goodies for the young men fighting over seas. One day, a man called me, asking if he could come to our meeting. I said yes, and gave him the time and the address. When he arrived, he presented us with a giant Mother's Day card, on which was addressed: TO OUR OTHER MOTHERS. The card was signed by all the men in his troop, in thanks for the boxes of gifts they had received from us. We never expected such a moving tribute.

Contributed by: Patti Alexander, former President of the American Legion #134, in Paramount, California. She now resides in Nebraska.

SLANTED POLITICS

I was student teaching in Roosevelt Junior High School in Bellflower, in 1968. I was teaching an 8th grade drafting class, on the day of the primary election for president. This was the year that Robert Kennedy was running on the Democratic Ticket, along with one or two other Democrats. Richard Nixon was running on the Republican ticket, along with one or two other Republicans. It was also the year that George Wallace was running on the American Independent party.

The kids came into class following the lunch break, and they were all hyped up about the election, probably from having listened to the news and their parents weigh in on the various candidates. I began the lesson in drafting for the day, but to no avail. The kids just wouldn't settle down, and were saying things that led me to believe that they thought we would "elect a new president today." So, recognizing that they would not pay attention to my prepared lesson, and recognizing that this was a "teachable moment," I departed from the days lesson plan.

I asked the class if they knew what a "primary" election was. Just as I suspected, they thought we would elect a new president that day. I taught them about our electoral system, and what a primary election is, and told them that if they wished, we could conduct a mock election in class. Of course, they were excited about this prospect. At the conclusion of the lesson, I devised paper ballots, and distributed two of them to each student, with the instruction that this would be a secret ballot, in which each student would have two votes: one on the Democratic ballot, and one on the Republican ballot. I wrote the names of all candidates on the board, separated by party affiliation. As the students began marking their ballots, one boy asked me how I would vote. I said that it didn't matter how I would vote, it only mattered how the class voted. He then asked me why Governor Wallace wasn't on the ballot. I explained that the American Independent party wasn't on the California ballot, and that we were using the candidates on our state ballot. The vote was completed and counted, with a winner in each of the major parties. I thought the students had learned about our primary system, as they enjoyed the lesson.

The next day, I was summoned to the principal's office, along with my master teacher. The principal asked about my lesson on "politics." I could see this wasn't going to go well. He showed me a letter from the father of the boy who had asked about Wallace, and about how I would vote. The letter accused me of being a communist, because I "forced" his son to tell me how he was going to vote, and I wouldn't tell him how I was going to vote, and I wouldn't let his son vote for George Wallace. Turns out, the father was the local school agitator. The principal was not happy with me, and told me to stick to my subject matter.

<u>Contributed by</u>: Richard Bonneau, after spending 12 years in the aerospace industry, he moved over to the Los Angeles Police Department. He is now a retired captain, after a 37 year career. He was assigned to seven patrol divisions, and worked a variety of assignments, including: vice enforcement, canine operations, Internal Affairs Division, and police academy instructor. As a captain, he has commanded Harbor Patrol Division, Scientific Investigation Division, including the department's crime lab.

PEOPLE ARE PEOPLE

After a lot of planning, fund raising, and the signing of permission slips, our Special Ed high school students embarked on a long weekend field trip to San Diego. It became clear that we would need more helpers to push the wheelchairs and help the students. Since I was already signed up—as the senior instructional aide—I asked my fiancé and my teenage daughter to help. Neither one had ever been even close to a handicapped person. While the other two teachers and I were loading the students on the buses, to drive to the airport, I looked around to see where my helpers were. They were standing together in a huddle, watching us, looking scared to death. We finally got everyone loaded, and off to the airport we went.

After the flight, as we disembarked at the San Diego airport, and retrieved our baggage, it became clear that the students needed to use the restroom. The only male to help the boys was my fiancé, so I told him to wait until I took the girls, and I would come back with instructions for the boys. He looked troubled. I told my daughter to watch over the remaining girls. She looked troubled, also.

As I was coming out of the restroom, anxious to find my troubled helpers, there was my fiancé in the middle of the boys, all laughing and having a good time. Wonderful!

And I found my daughter, walking down the hall, smiling and laughing with the girls. Wonderful!

The trip was to show those Special Ed teens things and places that they would probably never have the chance to see, otherwise; to enlarge their understandings; to widen their horizons. We went to the zoo. We went out to eat at a very nice restaurant. We stayed in a pleasant hotel. The San Diego School District provided the bus to take us around town. We even visited a Catholic Church on Sunday, before we flew home. These were all new experiences for them.

The students learned that there is an amazing world, filled with incredible people, beyond their school and home. And the teachable moment for both my fiance and my daughter was when they realized that people are people, regardless of their disabilities, and to overlook outside appearances. We all had a marvelous weekend.

Contributed by: Corrie Terry, who spent 15 years at Warren High School, in Paramount, as a Senior Instructional Aide for SMH (severely mentally handicapped), with her LVN (licensed vocational nurse) training. She retired when she and her husband moved to Placerville, and later to Bellflower, CA.

A Powerful Wish

While in the fifth grade, on a family road trip across the states, we were driving in the middle of nowhere, through a seemingly endless Arizona desert. Although the weather was clear, the car radio mentioned a chance of flash floods, and I excitedly said that I would *love* to see one, since I couldn't picture it in my mind. Mother became quite upset that I would say such a thing, and admonished me for doing so, ending with: "Be careful what you wish for!"

The sentence was barely out of her mouth, when, on cue, a powerful flash flood swept across the highway, washing the pickup truck in front of us off the road, landing it nose-down in a ditch. An enormous amount of water coursed around it, with such force that the doors couldn't be opened.

All traffic was stopped, unable to cross the dangerous fast-moving water, and we had a front row seat to the awesome destruction that a flash flood can wreak. I was further shocked to see that the driver of the truck was a young woman—gender issues were stuck in 1949—and that she had a small baby with her. Both were crying, so we didn't know if they were injured, or just freaking out about the unexpected situation. But we were unable to help.

Since cell phones were nonexistent at that time, someone had to turn around, and drive all the way back to the closest town, to get the sheriff. He and a helper finally arrived, with a heavier truck, ropes, and chains. We watched the ropes being used, as the sheriff battled through the water to rescue the baby first, and then went back to pull the woman to safety. Both were hauled out through the cab window. It was a long and arduous process. At length, the heavier truck pulled the pickup back onto the highway, and shortly thereafter, the flash flood had finally lost its punch. At that point, traffic was able to continue on, as if nothing had happened. Mother acted as if the whole experience was *my* fault, and I realized just how powerful our spoken words are.

HEALTH CLASS

I was teaching a freshman class in Health, and the subject was abortion. The students had very definite feelings: 13 were pro and 13 con, with four having a "whatever" response.

The class was divided into groups of four, to talk about their side of the issue. They became noisy, yelling at each other, and none were listening to the other side. So my homework assignment was that each had to do research, find jury trials, and interview people, on the *opposite* side of their chosen position. Then they would debate in class. The students were united: they were *furious!*

One girl, who was very, very, very, opposed to abortion, was so upset, that she started crying. She did not want to represent the other side of the issue.

After a few days for their individual research, they gathered on opposite sides of the room, and started debating. Boy! Did they do their homework! The debate got so noisy, and into somewhat of a yelling match, that I took them outside. I placed them on two mini-grassy knolls, with a walkway between. The directions were that they could not get off their hill, nor could they step onto the concrete path. They could yell all they wanted (since we were outside). It was amazing!

The upshot was that everyone learned about the opposing side of the issue. And the girl who was totally against abortion for any reason, told me that she had changed her stance a little: that cases of incest and rape were now causes for abortion, in her mind. The whole class was thrilled by their findings, and the education they received on the subject.

<u>Contributed by</u>: Sally Thompson, retired high school teacher, professional dancer, and university professor. She now lives in Corona, CA.

OLYMPIC PIN TRADING

It was 1988, in Seoul, Korea, at the Summer Olympic Games. While trading pins in Itaewon, a young man, who had been wandering around the booths, walked over to where I was set up, in front of a Dunkin' Doughnuts store. As he was looking over my pins, I noticed his competitor badge. "Are you a competitor?" I asked. He nodded yes, and I continued engaging him in small talk: "What do you do?" He said that he was on the Canadian Baseball Team, and played outfield. "How are you guys doing?" He murmured that they had lost that morning, and were now out of the competition. It became clear that he was just killing time in the shopping district, with nothing to do, and nowhere to go. He felt out-of-place, bored out of his mind, and had no money to speak of. "Do you have any Olympic pins?" I asked him. "No," he said, so I began telling him about them (Olympic team pins, sponsor pins, corporation pins, International Olympic Committee pins, badges, posters, and so forth). He sat down next to me, and watched as I traded or sold pins to passersby. At length, I asked, "Do you want to have some fun?" He was up for that, so I gave him a towel, and attached a bunch of pins to it, and told him to go trade or sell them. And away he went. A couple of hours later, he returned, all smiles.

He came back with a lot of different pins. I kept some that I didn't have, gave him the rest, and let him keep the money. He had a good time, and enjoyed interacting with people from around the world. Who knows? Maybe he still collects Olympic pins.

Contributed by: Wayne M. Meinberg, retired from Rancho Los Amigos Medical Center, after 30 years of service. He lives in Long Beach, CA.

Stolen, But Mysteriously Returned

I had attended an educational conference, on how to prevent children from stealing items in the classroom. I decided I would try the speaker's method.

Here is what she said to do: Gather the class and tell them about the missing item(s). Engage the class in a discussion of how the community and/or individuals would have to suffer, due to the item(s) that are missing. Be sure to allow students to participate in the discussion, adding their own experiences, suggestions, and other input. She also said to give them a chance to return the item(s) anonymously. She said to tell them that they could return the item as quietly and mysteriously as they took them, at any time.

In September of the following school year, I noticed some star reward stickers missing from my desk. I talked it over with my third grade class. No one knew what happened to the stickers. We talked about how no one would be able to receive those shiny, bright, gold, silver, green, red, and blue stickers for studying hard, or for a job well done, or achieving 100% on a spelling test. I didn't replace or give out any more stickers after that. Since it was a Catholic school, we mentioned how taking what is not ours is wrong, and against the fifth commandment of God.

I mentioned that since the person was able to sneak them away, that person could sneak them back anytime, including recess, lunch, or after school. And if that person just wanted to return them to me, there would be no questions asked, nor consequences.

The day went by, with no results. I reminded the class at dismissal time about the stickers. The next day, I discussed it again with the class. Some students volunteered additional information about it being wrong to take the stickers, and how the person couldn't use them in class, because everyone would know who took them. I also mentioned that, if he/she had already used the stickers, they could be replaced by buying more, or returning some money to buy new ones. Still no results. The next few days, I continued to remind the class, to no avail. I all but gave up on the idea.

A few months went by. Christmas time was drawing near, and the class was planning a Christmas party. The class decided to have a gift exchange, where everyone would draw a name, and give that classmate a present. As students often do, I also received some gifts, and cards, from students who could afford it.

There was one small gift wrapped in a white ribbon and shiny red wrapping paper, There was no name stating who the gift was from. I opened it, and to my surprise, low and behold, there was the box of stickers! Overjoyed, I told the class, and explained that they could once again receive stickers for their hard work. I also mentioned what a wonderful, creative way, in which the student chose to return the stickers. Later, after the class was dismissed, the student revealed her identity. I praised her for returning them in such a delightful manner, and for her courage to admit she had done it.

Contributed by: D.L. Laux. As a teacher and a freelance writer, she has worked in elementary schools as a substitute and a third grade teacher, a resource specialist, and a reading specialist. She has written articles for a syndicated newspaper service: "Helping Students Make the Grade," and "Christmas Customs of Other Countries." For the *Instructor* magazine, she wrote, "Whiz Quiz," regarding a learning game where students have fun learning various skills.

BIRTHDAY PARTY

As an adjunct professor at BYU one summer, I was working off-campus with a number of student teachers, in their last required all-day, four-week class, before certification. It was a show-and-tell experience, in which I presented tons of exciting projects to use in their own classrooms, to spice up otherwise dull subjects. Everyone eagerly participated in whatever lesson I presented, with much laughter and gusto involved. All became close to each other, with the exception of one older gentleman, who kept a reserved, dignified distance. He was obviously retired, and teaching was to be his second career. Besides having gray hair, he always wore a three-piece suit, with a long-sleeved white shirt, and formal-colored tie, while everyone else was dressed in colorful, casual summer outfits. So he not only looked, but acted, differently than his classmates. I was concerned that he hadn't jelled with the group, as easily or quickly as others had. I suspected that he came from a supervisory position, in some other field, and was unused to such familiarity and frivolity.

So, one fine, extremely HOT day, I happened to overhear a clerk mention that it was the gentleman's birthday. I decided to do something about it, in an effort to solidify his position in our class "family." Later that afternoon, I explained to the class that we were going on a walking field trip, and everyone enthusiastically followed me outside. They enjoyed their breezy walk (it was cooler outside than inside), and were quite surprised, as I led them to an ice cream parlor, several blocks hence. I explained that we were there in celebration of his birthday.

Everyone clapped and happily congratulated him, in one way or another, and we all spontaneously sang "Happy Birthday," as other customers joined in the festivities. The class was delighted, when I said that each person was to choose his/her own ice cream, as my treat, so we could all party together, on this special day. It was interesting to see all of the different flavor choices that were made, with much laughter and hilarity involved. As we were close to the end of our school day, the gentleman stood up before us, and began to thank us, but started *crying* instead. You can imagine how stunned we all were, to hear this older man say that he had *never* had a birthday party in his life, and it meant so much to him. You just never know how your actions will impact others.

LENGTHY LEARNING EXPERIENCES

Less often, a small teachable moment can turn into a full-blown unit of instruction, a longtime learning situation, a lifetime interest, or a hobby.

RUDE AND MOCKING REMARKS

As a junior in college, I was not paying an ounce of attention in the philosophy class that day. It was hot, and I was not focusing on the dull and boring delivery of the subject at hand. I was simply zoning out—in a dreamlike state—when I heard the instructor say, ". . . and of course, there is *reincarnation*," whereupon the entire class began to loudly jeer and derisively laugh. That sure caught my attention. *What was that word again? Why did everyone else know about it, and I hadn't a clue? Why was the whole class being so negative? What was so unusually odd about it, that would cause such an instant uproar?* So, being curious, I later moved my inquiring mind to the library, where I began researching the subject. In those days, it was difficult to find any such information in the libraries or bookstores, but I persevered. As a result of such questioning about *one* unknown word, my independent study of reincarnation has taken over 55 years, to date. I find the concept to be incredibly fascinating!

LONG-RANGE GOAL

Scotty was a pasty-white, sumo-sized third grader (nicknamed the Michelin Man, and also the Stay-Puft marshmallow Man, after he sat on a sink in the Boy's Room and broke it off the wall). He was totally uninterested in learning to read. He vowed and declared that he had no reason to read, because his goal in life was to be a TV wrestler. And he had the strength and size to succeed at it.

Knowing nothing about wrestling, I researched the subject, and found that the only wrestling school in the country was in Northern California. So I contacted the school, asking for the requirements, and had them send me an application package.

I gave the material to Scotty, explaining that the first requirement for entrance to the wrestling school was a high school diploma. So he had to learn to read, in order to complete his education, and achieve his ultimate goal. And besides, I explained, he'd need to be able to read his contract. Then I bought a little paperback book about wrestling, as further motivation for him to learn to read. It had pictures of all his favorite wrestlers on the left-hand pages, with biographical information about them on the facing page. I told Scotty that he could have the book, when he could read it aloud to me. He was totally stoked, and learned by leaps and bounds.

ONE MORE TIME

I had hired an internal transfer for a position that was nonunion, coming from a union shop. His current supervisor recommended not hiring him, saying that he had a bad attitude, and was a trouble-maker, with poor attendance. I had a gut feeling, and hired him anyway. I decided to do the training myself, instead of the lead, because I wanted to ensure that he was given a fair shot. He was extremely nervous with me doing the training. After he had asked me the same question a couple of times, he was visibly upset to have to ask it again. I said, "Ask as many times as you need. My job is to make you successful, and we will do whatever it takes." He was quiet for a moment, and then said, "You really mean that, don't you?" When I answered yes, he actually got tears in his eyes, and told me that he had never had a manager who cared anything about him as a person. He turned out to be a dynamic team member, and was honored again and again for customer service.

Contributed by: Maggie L. Headrick, retired from Kaiser Permanente for over 40 years. Her specialty was Information, Technology, Payroll, and Human Resources. She now lives in Highlands Ranch, Colorado.

Immigration

One much-loved Lakewood High School history student teacher (under long contract), related the following personal incident during a lecture on Martin Luther King, Jr. and the civil rights movement, to his 11th grade students:

The student teacher had immigrated to the USA when he was six years old, and was immediately placed in the first grade, late in the school year. He knew no English whatsoever, and his teacher knew only a few Spanish words, so he rarely understood what was going on.

Each class was participating in a program for the PTA. Parents were invited to attend the presentation in the auditorium. His teacher, naturally wanting all her students to be included in their play, gave him the only *nonspeaking* part. She pinned a star on his chest, as he was to be a policeman, and modeled his job. All he had to do was walk across the stage, grab a girl by the arm, and drag her off the stage. As a first grader, he was apprehensive about being on display in front of all those strangers—not only kids, but adults, too. Not knowing *why* he was told to do what he was to do was the worst of it, but it seemed an easy enough thing to accomplish.

Unfortunately for him, when he walked across the stage and grabbed the girl's arm (who was representing Rosa Parks), everyone started booing. He thought the audience didn't like him, and he began to cry in the middle of the performance. He didn't know what he had done wrong! It was years before he realized that the audience had been booing the *historical situation*, and not him personally. What a way to be introduced to civil rights!

The teacher's story bridged the gap between a few stilted textbook paragraphs and a meaningful connection to history. The impact on the class was immediate. The room was suddenly buzzing. The students were filled with compassion, and saddened by their teacher's childhood situation, and were trading constant comments: "Oooh, our teacher is an immigrant", "He wasn't born here?", "Is he an illegal immigrant?" and similar words to that affect. The students had such empathy for him. Concerned questions swirled around the room, which made the perfect beginning for a unit of study about Immigration.

VERY BAD DAY

In 1972, the children's book, *Alexander and the Terrible, Horrible, No Good, Very Bad Day*, by Judith Viorst, was first published. I read a preview about it in *Psychology Today* magazine. When no bookstores had it in stock yet, I tried to order it. The owner of the bookstore laughed in a very unpleasant way, telling me there was no such book with that *ridiculous* title, and curtly dismissed me. I was obviously wasting his time. Standing my ground, I argued with him, and a crowd of onlookers formed around us, listening to our conversation. I was well-known in the Long Beach Unified School District, as an expert in Children's Literature, as I was always presenting show-and-tell speeches in various schools and conventions, so the teachers in the crowd were enjoying our debate. (Years later, I taught kiddy lit courses at two universities, which was my favorite subject.) I finally convinced him to order one. He was amazed to find that there *was* such a title. And because I was ordering it, others did also. Later, when I went back to pick it up, he had shown a change of heart. He told me that every time I ordered a new title, he would order a dozen copies, because he knew they were going to sell. We established a good relationship thereafter, over the unusual title of a book. How weird is that?

[All these decades later, *Alexander and the Terrible, Horrible, No Good, Very Bad Day* continues to be a best-selling children's classic. A movie was made, based on the book and title (2014), via the Walt Disney Pictures and the Jim Henson Company.]

MUSIC APPRECIATION

When I was in the Santa Monica school system in the 1950s, I took Music Appreciation, hoping that the class would be an hour of r&b and rock n' roll music. Instead, the experience turned out to be one of the defining moments in my life.

On our first day of class, there stood a lanky young man with glasses and a baton. Donald Richardson welcomed us. Without saying a word, he walked over to the record player, and put the needle on the beginning track of an album. Mr. Richardson walked back to his desk, stepped up on his chair, and then onto his desk. All of a sudden Rimsky-Korsakov's "Scheherazade" oozes into the room. For a half hour, the piece consumed our classroom and our teacher/conductor.

To this day, the mere mention of Rimsky-Korsakov sends me back in a zooming time machine, to see Mr. Richardson perched on his desk, immersed in conducting an imaginary orchestra.

I never got hooked on classical music, but the startling introduction by Mr. Richardson, gave me a musical appreciation that lasts to this day, not only for music, but how one teacher can make a difference. He went on to be the music guru for the entire Santa Monica School District.

Contributed by: Dan Barrett. Reprinted with permission. Publisher of Internet radio news site, LARadio.com. Authored: *Los Angeles Radio People* (1997).

A Different Approach

I managed a telephone operator who was known to be rude to our patients and staff. Previous managers had not dealt with the problem, because she happened to be the only minority in the group. I called her into my office for *discipline*, as she sat down. But then I decided to go in a whole different direction, and asked her what would be her ideal job. She acted confused, and asked "Why?"

I said, "I think you are really sharp, and that you are underemployed. You become bored and impatient, and end up being rude to others. I do not believe that to be your intention. I just think you are underemployed. What would you prefer to be doing?" Adding, "I am not going to fire you. I just want to help you grow."

She appeared shocked, and shared that she had always been interested in law, but could not afford to go to school. I told her about the company education assistance plan, and further recommended a women's group for professional black women, and offered to help her in any way. She was never again rude, that I am aware of, and she did end up getting a paralegal certificate.

Contributed by: Maggie L. Headrick, retired from Kaiser Permanente for over 40 years. Her specialty was Information, Technology, Payroll, and Human Resources. She now lives in Highlands Ranch, Colorado.

PUNCTUATION

My father was born in a sod house, in the Oklahoma territory, before statehood. As such, he had little schooling at first. Individuals who were sixteen years old were allowed to teach, so as a child, his education was hit and miss. When the family moved closer to a town, he arrived at a new school, and as asked to read aloud. He was prideful of his ability to read at a rapid rate. Which he did. Thereafter, the wide-eyed and open-mouthed students erupted into hysterical laughter. He was stunned, and highly embarrassed, not knowing the cause of the hilarity. It turned out that he had never learned about punctuation, and never knew to stop at a period. He just plowed through word after word, with no meaning or expression involved. Many years later, surprisingly—during the Depression— he graduated from college with a teaching credential. He became an educator, teaching mostly English (grammar and punctuation skills). He became a principal, and then superintendent in Oklahoma. He taught aviation cadets in WWII, and was stationed in California when the war ended. He continued teaching in California, until he retired. Punctuation is not just a trifling matter.

WHISTLEBLOWER

My motivation was pure. I felt a moral responsibility to try to right the wrongs that I saw in my local public schools. As a result, I wrote my first book, *Into the Hornet's Nest: An Incredible Look at Life in an Inner City School* (1993). My innocent desire was that if the public was aware of the educational problems therein, we could all work together to fix them. Wrong. I was shocked and dumbfounded at the huge and lasting response. It had a divisive impact, that I couldn't have foreseen: the book clearly divided the district.

The teachers thought that I was the best thing since sliced bread, and the administrators thought of me as a traitor. And I was shunned, because, as one administrator put it, "I had held out the district's dirty laundry for everyone to see." It was not a pleasant experience.

Decades later, retiring after 34 years teaching, I became a professor at National University, in a different county. Over the course of my 16 years there, I had three adult students, who had checked out of my classes, because their parents had been administrators in the district, when my book had been published. (I did not know their parents, but the taint still stood.) Even though I considered my efforts to be righteous, the repercussions persisted. Over the decades, various individuals have suggested that I reprint my first book, which is certainly validating. But, even though I have written thirteen books now, and have been honored with well over one hundred awards, every now and then, someone from the good old days, will say, upon first meeting me, "Oh, you wrote *that* book!"

NIGHTMARE

We had a new hire. The office needed a Spanish-speaking person, so the boss hired Gloria. Now I am always cheerful in the morning, and generally speaking, I would describe myself as being "Pollyanna-ish," if you know what I mean. You'd be surprised how many co-workers didn't appreciate that. O.K., maybe they're just not morning people.

As I got to know Gloria, she commenced telling me that she grew up in the mean streets of south central L.A. Razor blades hidden in her hair, and the whole bit. Not a very nice person, at all. And she made it clear that she did not like me, AT ALL. I was too nice for her liking, and not what she was used to. I was actually afraid to walk out to my car after work. She *hated* me! Gee, I never really had anyone hate me before.

Well, a little backstory: My wonderful son, Mark, was in his sophomore year, and went to live with his dad, in Oregon. While there, he got mixed up with drugs, and other sorts of nefarious activity. I was devastated, thinking that I should never have let him move to Oregon. I was so worried, just beside myself.

One night, I had a nightmare. I dreamt that I went to visit Mark in jail, and an officer said, "Sorry, we had to execute him." I cried, and screamed, and wanted answers. I sat in the hall on a bench. My crying demanded answers, but no one heard my pleas. NO ONE!

Then, out of nowhere, Gloria appeared. She embraced me, and told me that it would be okay, and that she knew how I felt. She was sweet and tender.

The next day I woke up. Thank God it was just a bad nightmare. So that morning at work, I said to Gloria, "I had a nightmare last night, and you were in it." She was getting ready to defend herself, and meet me in the parking lot. As I sat at my desk, with my co-workers all around, I explained my nightmare, and how Gloria was the only one who came to comfort me. I said, "Thank you, Gloria," as tears came into my eyes. She came over and gave me a tight hug, as tears came to her eyes. Her defenses melted, and she felt wonderful, and so did I. We had a new respect for each other, and we've been good friends ever since. I'll never forget her.

And my son, Mark, is awesome now.

Contributed by: Marsha P. Reeder, retired from clerking in the Orange County Superior Court in California, when she moved to Oregon.

MICE!

I was teaching a dance class in the High School Performing Arts Complex that had become infested with mice. Students would spot two or three mice scampering around, which set them off with a series of screams, running around and scaring themselves. The custodians would place mouse traps all over the area, to no avail. The mice were smart! Everyone could hear the snap of the traps, but the mice enjoyed the food, without getting caught.

One day, the class was sitting on the floor, watching the dancers on the stage, when a mouse chose to sit about two feet away from a girl. It was sitting upright, on its haunches. Both were raptly staring at the dancers. I watched in fascination, preparing myself for the expected response. To my dismay, she turned around, stared at the mouse, and turned back to watch the rest of the dance.

When the dance was finished, to my surprise, the girl turned around, both mouse and girl saw each other, and NOTHING! The mouse sauntered off. No response from the girl.

Eventually, the custodians used sticky cardboards to catch the mice, but by that time, everyone was living in peace with each other.

<u>Contributed by</u>: Sally Thompson, retired high school teacher, dance instructor, and university professor. She now lives in Riverside County, CA.

SERIOUS DRAMA

Angel Street was a very serious drama, with deep psychological issues, dealing with induced insanity and a carefully planned plot to drive the female lead out of her mind. The goal of the play was to draw the mystery-loving audience into the intrigue by slowly building tension and suspense in a hushed auditorium.

The actor that played the Charles Boyer character insisted on wearing a glued-on mustache, and sideburns applied with eyebrow pencil, in order to look properly sinister. Unfortunately, the mustache came unstuck on one side of his upper lip, perhaps due to nervous perspiration. The Bergman character was named Bella, and each time he yelled *"Bella!"* which he did frequently, the right side of his prop mustache blew forward. Always in character, he maintained his composure as the audience began to snicker.

Later on in the scene, Bella gave him a big hug, and one of the black, painted-on sideburns transferred to her cheek. Whenever she turned that side of her face to the audience, the laughter surged.

Then the maid brought in a tray of teacups and saucers. She inadvertently placed it precariously on the edge of the coffee table, half on and half off. The shaky floor of the stage and the action of the actors rushing back and forth rattled and teetered the tray with every move. The audience gasped every time it tipped. She kept loading and removing full and empty cups, first on the table side, and then on the off-side of the tray. The audience sat on the edge of their seats. They talked and chuckled among themselves with their eyes glued on the shaking tray, breathlessly waiting for it to fall, which it never did.

Another performer, handsome and with a beautifully dramatic voice, had become known for never being able to memorize the volume of words needed for major parts. Nevertheless, he was cast as one of the leads. He solved his problem by typing out his lines, and taping them onto the props, the furniture, on his left and right sleeves, writing them on his hands, or inside his hat.

With great, characteristic flair, he strode confidently from the wings, and delivered one line after another flawlessly. As his part continued, however, he slowly began to lose his poise as he searched the stage furniture and props for his next line. He completely lost track of where his lines were, and finally just started using the script that was in his pocket, much to the added amusement of the audience.

At one point, he needed to open a locked drawer. Trying to hold a flashlight in the semi-darkness with one hand, and the key in the other, he had no hand to hold the script. His desperate fussing and fumbling was not lost on the audience, who by that time was convinced this was one of the best comedy/melodramas they'd ever seen.

With the blowing of the mustache with each *"Bella;"* the tray of cups rocking but never tumbling; and an actor hunting frantically all over the stage for his next line—the audience laughter grew from the opening to the final curtain—much to the surprise and confusion of the poor director. He had thought, through all of the rehearsals, that this was a mystery/drama. From where he stood backstage, when the audience was supposed to gasp with horror, instead he heard them roar with laughter. Only the players and the audience knew why, and they would never tell him.

Many of the members of that cast went on to careers in the theatre or to teach drama. I'm sure they've all learned and passed on an important lesson—sometimes chaos, minor disasters, accidents, and imperfections can create memorable moments in the theatre, and incidently, some of the most delightful entertainment. They shouldn't be taken too seriously. It often makes life more interesting.

<u>Contributed by</u>: Reprinted with permission from Patty Palmer Weckbaugh in *Chopped Liver for the American Spirit* anthology. She is the President of the Book Publicists of Southern California (BPSC).

SPLASH!

Way back, when I was around eleven or twelve years old, and my brother was probably six or so, we were in the kitchen doing our chores. I was washing the dishes, and he was supposed to be drying them. He kept bugging me about something, and wasn't doing his job. I do not recall what he was doing, but I kept telling him to stop, and he didn't. We were making a lot of noise. I was so angry that I started threatening him, saying that if he didn't stop, I was going to throw the pan of water on him. But he didn't stop. And I was so incensed that I *did* throw the pan of water on him! And he was *drenched*, and water was all over the floor. We were both shocked into silence, as we stared at each other. Then we started whispering, that we had to quickly clean up the floor, because Mom and Dad would get mad. (Of course, they were both in the living room, and had heard the whole shouting match, but let us take care of the problem ourselves, without interfering.)

I always thought of this experience as only a way we had dodged a bullet, by avoiding a tongue-lashing and possibly further repercussions (restriction or a loss of a weekly allowance). And never gave it much thought, other than relief. Over fifty years later, however, I found that my little brother (who was brilliant even then!) had considered this well-remembered event as *life-changing*, as it was the first time we had collaborated to avoid conflict. It was pivotal in seeing that anger issues and emotional explosions often get in the way of sensible resolutions. Decades afterward, as a leader (he founded and ran a number of businesses and corporations within 37 countries), he realized that nothing is more stressful and emotionally draining, than a full-blown argument (whether with an angry family member—me!—or an acting out friend, or an aggressive subordinate, or an unruly customer). He had learned, early on—from our little experience—that conflict management was a valuable tool.

REPEATED REFRAIN

A high school student, who had graduated five years earlier, made a point of coming back to the school to visit me. She made it very clear that I had been responsible for her graduating from college, and was now teaching English to Spanish-speaking students at the University of Mexico! Like what? *What did I say?* I was her dance teacher!

Seems that when she went on to junior college with the rest of her friends, after their classes, everyone would get together, and say, "Let's go to the beach," or "Let's go to the park," or "Let's go . . . wherever!" The former dance student, however, kept hearing the words whenever I gave an assignment: "Get your dance homework done as soon as possible! Then practice it!" As a result, she would tell everyone that she would meet them later. Then she went home, did her homework, and found that it took until 9:00 P.M., most of the time, to complete her work. As a result, she rarely met with them for whatever. They, in turn, came home late, and couldn't finish the homework on time. Her friends were dropped from classes, and flunked the semester. Those that lasted at all, never made it through the second year. She went on to graduate from a four-year college, always hearing the words: "Get your work done first, then play."

<u>Contributed by</u>: Sally Thompson, retired high school teacher, professional dancer, and university professor.

My First Trip To The Drags

After a long week of digging swimming pools in the early 60's, I was invited to go with a coworker, to Lion's Drag Strip. Over the last year, on many occasions, he told me how much fun he was having, helping a friend with his race car. So I went with him one Saturday. On our way to Lion's, we stopped at Wilcaps, in Torrance, to pick up some Nitro. I was so clueless, I thought it was solvent, and that we were going to clean some parts with it. As we approached the main gate, I could hear the cars racing down the strip. I watched in awe as we entered, just as a dragster was warming up, coming down the push start area. Wow! The noise just blew me away! My first whiff of Nitro. Unbelievable! It attacked my senses, burning my eyes, and shaking my body. It was thrilling! We headed over to the pits to find his friend, while passing many beautiful dragsters on the way. I was really starting to like this, as we pulled up next to a tilt trailer with a roadster on it. "That's it!" he said, as a smiling young man came over to greet us. "Hi, my name is Gary Cochran." The tank of the race car was filled, and we set off pushing it down the start-up road to warm the motor. I was able to help that day, instead of sitting in the stands. Wow! We qualified, and lost in the first round, but I was hooked. In those days, it was a low budget affair, and everyone worked out in their garages, having too much fun. Everyone was friendly, and helped each other, while doing a lot of bench racing. Unexpectedly, that first day was a whole new learning experience—and the beginning of my long love affair with drag racing. And I became a permanent crew member of Gary Cochran's Mr. C Roadster. And all these years later, most of those early weekend warriors are in the Hall of Fame, and the Who's Who of Drag Racing. And I became a multi-year President of the Lakewood Lions Club, and a board member of the Lion's Drag Strip.

Contributed by: Wayne M. Meinberg, retired from Rancho Los Amigos Medical Center, after 30 years of service. He lives in Long Beach, CA.

CAMPING SPACE

While living in Placerville, in beautiful Northern California, my husband and I would turn our humongous front yard into a camping space for cross country runners, from Paramount's Warren High School (the school in which I used to teach, before moving some 400 miles distant). The boys would come in August, and spend three weeks, camping with their tents and sleeping bags. Each day, they would go out to train—walking, running at a slow, easy pace, then jogging, and finally hill sprinting— through the beautiful trees, and by the lake, filling their lungs with clean air. Oddly, every boy had at least a 3.5 or above GPA. There was one that held a 5.0 for the four years he was with us. Amazing!! (That was a big learning moment for me, as I always had the idea that students who went out for track were there because they had to pick something, and track was a sport in which they didn't have to do too much.)

We enjoyed these visits greatly. The learning moment would come every year for the boys at the end of their stay. We would all sit around in a circle, and they, one by one, would say how much they enjoyed our hospitality, and what they learned from their outdoor experience. There was always at least one boy that would ask how we could give up our property and peace and quiet, and put up with all 12 to 15 boys for so long a time, each year. We would then explain that we did it so that they could get good training and conditioning, and that we loved having them.

It was a wonderful ten year experience. In 2013, the boys won CIF, and went on to the State Finals, where they came in 4th place. We are happy to have been a part of their training.

<u>Contributed by</u>: Corrie Terry, who spent 15 years teaching at Warren High School, in Paramount, CA. She retired when she and her husband moved to Placerville, in Northern California, for a number of years. They have since moved to Bellflower.

Lock Your Doors!

About 7:20 one Sunday morning, I had just walked through the park, and didn't see any squirrels, so I was placing peanuts in the crevices of the tree trunk in our front yard. I heard a commotion, and turned around, to see a young woman (maybe 25 years of age), running out the front door of our house, with my husband shouting right behind her. He was in his shorts, so he skidded to a stop at the edge of the porch, as he yelled to me that the gal was in our bedroom. She had leaned over him, as he slept, looking into his face. He opened his eyes, and upon seeing a stranger's face directly above him, freaked out, and yelled, "What are you doing here?" She yelled, "Sorry!" and ran out of the room, through the library, all the way down the hall, through the living room, and out the front door. Upon seeing me, he yelled, "Catch her!" and ran back into the house to call 911, and put some clothes on. In the meantime, I chased the girl, and cornered her between a wall and a car next door, and asked what she was doing. She just kept moaning, "I want to go home, I want to go home."

I asked her where she lived, and she said, "L.A." Since we were in Long Beach, she was quite a ways from her home in Los Angeles. Darlene, our neighbor, seemed to know her, and I thought this gal might be an undesirable relative, from her attitude towards the girl. Darlene sternly directed her to sit down on the porch bench, as she went inside to get her some food. I thought it a peculiar response, until I later got the story from Darlene, alongside two neighbors on the other side of our house.

It seems that Darlene's 22-year-old son, had a BLIND DATE. Apparently, she drank. A lot. She was so totally inebriated, that she ended up urinating and vomiting all over her clothes, and his sheets and carpet, in the middle of the night. Darlene was so irritated, because she had to clean up the mess, since the girl was in no condition to do so. Darlene told her to go sit on the porch bench (because the stench was so bad), and wait for them to come outside. The gal got tired of waiting, apparently, and walked off the porch, falling down on the grass, and breaking several porcelain lawn ornaments in the process. She then ran across our front lawn, and over to our neighbor's house on the other side. When she couldn't wake anyone (they sleep upstairs in the back), she climbed in their unlocked green, classic Bullet Mustang, and fell asleep. When Darlene and her son finally finished cleaning up his room, the girl was nowhere to be found. They searched the neighborhood high and low, and finally called it a night. Much later, although still dark outside, the girl woke up, and rang their doorbell of the second house, again, asking for a ride home. When she told them that she lived in L.A., they decided to call a cab for her, but cabs are unavailable so early in the morning. (Who knew?) So the gal came over to our house. She rang our doorbell, and when no one answered, she went right on inside. She turned the lights on in each room, as she went through. (I thought she might have been casing the joint, since I always make sure all the lights are off, when I leave for my walks). But no, she was simply looking for something familiar.

So *five* (count them: one, two, three, four, five!) squad cars arrived for this drunk woman (when I couldn't get *any* to come for me, in my stalking—life or death—situation! But I digress.) They just missed talking to the son, who had taken her back to the house party where he had found her, originally. Anyway, the police talked to all of us, and didn't leave until an hour later. The crux of the matter is that trespassing is not a felony, so there wasn't much to be done about it. (We were told to just be thankful that she didn't have a butcher knife!) Two squad cars did wait around until he finally came home, and questioned him at length, but the gal also told him that she lived in L.A., and was visiting with friends in Long Beach. I don't think he knew more than her first name (if it was her real name, anyway), since they only knew each other from Facebook. He later complained that she didn't even look like her picture. (Duh. Have a clue!) Oh, well, a little excitement on a Sunday morning.

Our unusual experience reminded everyone in our surrounding neighborhood—and city—to LOCK YOUR DOORS!

INSPIRED

I have always had stories to write and tell, but what really inspired me to publish my work was the author of the *Inheritance Cycle*, Christopher Paolini. While reading his books, and researching his bio, I realized he was a teenager, who had published his first book at a young age. When I discovered this fact, I was in middle school, and experimenting with various genres to find one what suited me the best, while struggling with the many challenges my autism caused me. However, after hearing about Paolini from one of my aides, I decided I should focus on sharing my stories with the rest of the world through publishing my work. I thought that if a young man with humble beginnings could accomplish so much at such a youthful age, then an Aspergers person, like me, could do the same. With Paolini's background in mind, I sought to not just publish my work while I was still young, but also prove that others who have neurodevelopment disorder issues, like me, could pursue their dreams like a normal person could. It was because of the background content of Christopher Paolini's origin that I was able to push myself, and my work, as far as I did: writing the first book in my series as a senior in high school, and the second while in college, and the third shortly after graduation.

Dr. Sherry L. Meinberg

<u>Contributed by</u>: Grady P. Brown, author of the sci/fi series: *The Young Guardians and the Genesis Spell* (2009); *The Young Guardians and the Great Darkness* (2012); and *The Young Guardians and the Revelation Orb* (2015). He lives in Tustin, CA.

A MINDSET CHANGE

I always wanted to be a teacher. I was surrounded my teachers. Both my mother and father were teachers, as were several aunts, uncles, and cousins. My next-door neighbor was a school counselor, the lady across the street was a high school teacher, and a substitute teacher lived at the end of our cul-de-sac. In the second grade, I made little books for all my dolls, and before I went to school each morning, I dressed my dolls, and put them on my bed with their books, which I pretended was their school. I told them that I was going to work as a teacher at my school. While in middle school and high school, I would critique my teachers, during their daily lessons, mentally applauding them when they taught something well. I knew what they could have said or done to interest the various subgroups of students (the sports-minded, the popular kids, the nerds, the "bad boys", and even those who had no interest whatsoever in school), to get them to participate.

Although I longed to be a teacher, I somehow got the message over the years, that I wasn't cut out for it, as my parents were reserved, formal, and serious. My daily role-models were not given to frivolity. And I was bold, highly creative, and living out loud: I liked to play and laugh, dance and sing, and simply share the joy of living. I thought I was "too different" from them, which I felt didn't go hand-in-hand with the role of an educator. As such, since I had studied ballet, toe, and tap dancing for 15 years, I decided that a career in the theatre was most likely for me. My girlfriend was a year older, and had already graduated from high school, and had signed a dancing contract, and I was set to follow in her footsteps. We had it all planned out. (The fact that the livelihood of a dancer is the most meager of all performing artists never even crossed my mind.)

When I was a senior in high school (1956/7), just before Christmas, my parents hosted a holiday party. They had never held a party before (or since). *They didn't even go to parties!* They only rarely interacted with neighbors. A few of their teacher friends arrived early, just as my younger brother and I were leaving. Neither of us knew anything about the party! We both had separate things planned for the evening, but we stayed outside in the dark, staring in the windows, at all of the strangers. We stood transfixed, absolutely dumbfounded, as many bottles of liquor were carried through the door. We couldn't believe our eyes! They were all having such a good time, singing and dancing and eating. The shocker was that they were also *drinking!* Now we had been raised in a teetotaler household (no drinking, no smoking, no gambling, no swearing, no carousing, no drugs, and no nonsense allowed). Total abstinence. So this behavior was surprising and dismaying. Both of us were taken aback at what we were witnessing.

So we decided to stick around for a bit. We watched the teachers—strangers from two different districts, and two different grade levels, elementary and middle school—happily carrying on together, and obviously having a good time. A smaller group was gathered around the piano in the dining room, singing their hearts out, when Mother decided, for some unknown reason, that she wanted the piano moved into the living room. My brother and I watched in amazement, as four burly guys lifted the piano, and carefully moved it into the spot Mother had indicated, as the cluster of carolers moved along with them, singing in unison, while the piano player continued pounding on the keys, without skipping a beat. All were in a cheerful mood. Laughter was bouncing off the walls, and reverberating through the house. How unusual! It was a mesmerizing experience. My brother and I couldn't get over the fact that these were *teachers* who were drinking, smoking, and loudly enjoying themselves. They were behaving just like regular people! The situation deeply affected both of us.

While looking through the window, I made a momentous *aha!* discovery: Teachers could actually have *fun!* They could be noisy and excited! They could laugh, and sing. They could party on! At that pivotal moment, I changed the direction of my whole life. In one fell swoop, I followed my heart, and danced my last dance. I discarded my dancing career, and resolved to attend college, and become a teacher. And I did—and happily, passionately, taught—for over fifty years!

I find it remarkable, that by observing that one unexpected party, my life was profoundly altered. It staggers the imagination.

Manzanar

Since the early 50s, as a family, we had driven up Highway 395 to the High Sierras, every year, for the Opening Day of trout season. Over those years, we went from campfires to condos, as our financial situation changed. Each time we passed Manzanar, Mother would always explain how that was the place in which local Japanese were *unjustly* incarcerated during WWII. It was one of ten camps, across the nation, in which over 10,000 citizens were forced to relocate. It is considered to be the best-preserved of the former campsites, and is now called the Manzanar National Historic Site.

Later, in the 80s, while working at Rancho Los Amigos Hospital, I met a Japanese-American that volunteered for a study with a new type of artificial leg. He had lost his leg in Italy in WWII, while fighting with the 442 (the all Japanese-American unit). We often talked about fishing, and the drive north on Highway 395. He told me that he had been in Manzanar (the Japanese internment camp), at the start of the war. He then volunteered for the 442nd Infantry Regimental Combat Team, and was shipped out of state, and later to Italy. As a war buff, I learned so much about his experiences, and it was a really big deal for me, to hear about the most decorated unit in U.S. military history. It was awarded eight Presidential Unit Citations and 21 of its members were awarded the Medal of Honor.

On his last visit to follow up on his new artificial leg, he brought me a large felt pennant that read CAMP SHELBY—HOME OF THE 442, and gave it to me. Wow! I felt so honored, and expressed my thanks. I kept it for years, until I read that Manzanar was looking for items to place in their brand new museum. Then I took the pennant with me, on one of my yearly trout fishing trips, and stopped at Manzanar. I donated the pennant to one of the curators, who was very excited about it. So it had a new home. It had come full circle.

Contributed by: Wayne M. Meinberg, retired, but still fishing.

THANKS, DAD!

My father ingrained in me, at a very early age, that girls could do anything, and be anything they wanted . . . no restrictions! As a result, I frequently gave my female students this same advice.

One girl amazed me, after she graduated from high school. She made a point of having me come to her 10-year reunion. She informed me that due to my constant saying she could do and be anything she wanted, she now owned two fitness centers, and was building a third, all by herself.

This was amazing to me, because she had been the treasurer of the Dance Club in her senior year, and proceeded to count all the money from a fund raiser, by sitting on the floor, and piling money on the rug, into a growing mountain! This was no neat little pile of quarters, dimes, nickels, etc. Nooo. Just mixed coin on top of coin, willy-nilly, like cairns rock stacks. How did she possibly know how much money she had counted?

That same girl is now independent, self-sufficient, and definitely very together!

Yay, for Dad! And, yes. Girls CAN do anything!

<u>Contributed by</u>: Sally Thompson, retired high school teacher, professional dancer, and university professor.

THE COCKROACH INVASION

Through the years, intermittently, I'd remember an incident that happened in my third grade classroom, and I laughed every time I thought about it. Finally, I decided to share the fun. So I wrote a children's book, *The Cockroach Invasion*. It chronicles the exciting and scary experience of the time that hundreds upon hundreds of cockroaches exploded out of Room 8's classroom sink. We thought an oil derrick had sprung a leak, causing a black geyser, until the cockroaches hit the floor, and began skittering around! Mass pandemonium ensued, as you can well imagine.

When I told my friends and family that I was writing the story, they were not supportive, in the least. Their facial expressions and negative comments were off-the-charts. (They looked like they had swallowed vinegar.) No one shared my vision. But I persevered anyway. I knew the subject matter for adults was a complete and total turn-off, but children love the yuck factor. So I thought it might have a slight chance at readership.

After I wrote it, I couldn't find any professional artists to do the illustrations. None wanted to be connected to cockroaches in any way, shape, form, or fashion. At length, I held a contest for third and fourth graders, and the winners were from different schools in different cities. I actually like their sketches better, since the story is about youngsters, after all.

After *The Cockroach Invasion* was published (2014), the book received a lot of local publicity, and within the first six months, it had received ten awards. (I was amazed!) Fan mail arrived from various states, and countries. Now I am having so much fun with the book, and I am greeted with smiles. It turns out that everyone has a cockroach story to tell me. I've been happily introduced as "The Cockroach Lady," and "Dr. Cockroach," and as "an expert in the field." Awareness has been raised, which was my intention. Instead of cockroaches being seen as gross and icky, they are now being seen as utterly fascinating. *How fun is that?!*

Dad's 'Teaching Moments' Finally Starting to Pay Off

My parents had a rule when I was growing up: we couldn't drive until we could afford to pay our own car insurance.

At the broke age of 15, parting with 100 bucks a month "in case" something happened—because I was sure nothing would—not only seemed stupid, but insurmountable. Until that point, my meager income from baby-sitting and relatives at birthdays and Christmas, went to pay for Guess jeans and eggnog, the only things I can remember being important to me at the time.

But I really, really wanted to drive. So I got a ride from my mom to the outlet mall—she dropped me off at the Applebee's across the street, to avoid the embarrassment of dependence—and landed a retail job at a baby clothing store, which gave me a new goal: Go to college and get a career, so I never again have to listen to the techno version of "Deck the Halls" for eight hours a day, nor find piles of soiled diapers in fitting rooms.

I paid my car insurance, insisting I knew everything there was to know about driving, and within a month had actually accumulated two traffic tickets and had caused a minor finder bender; not long afterward, my brother was broadsided in his '66 Mustang, totaling it. Our parents seized on these "valuable teaching moments."

The resentment of their smugness stung again, two decades later, when the rebellious backbone of my being cringed at their insistence I perchance homeowners insurance for my condo. Six hundred dollars a year. I mentally tallied all the things I could do with that kind of money, knowing the likelihood was greater that it would be piddled away in dozens of bored trips to Target, rather than be socked away for some exotic vacation.

But after the sixth time my dad asked, at the end of our weekly phone conversations, whether I had called the insurance company—he had gotten the name and number for me, which didn't help my motivation—I wrote the check.

And, alas, the rains that dumped on Southern California last week, welcomed yet another teaching moment into my life.

I woke at 4 a.m. to the sight of J.J. on his hands and knees, maneuvering a tapestry of towels over the dining room floor, barking out orders to no one in particular. Water was pooled everywhere, squishing from the cracks of my hardwood floors.

I went back to bed. His daughter, Zoe, didn't even stir.

At a more responsible hour, and several cups of coffee later, J.J. had identified the cause as a backed-up storm drain outside, and had compiled a list of phone numbers to call and tasks to do. Immediately.

We would have to hire a company to dry the floors, which will have to be replaced, given the wood was already buckling.

Christmas, it seemed, would have to be canceled this year. Early estimates for the fix are more than $5,000.

"You have insurance, right?" he demanded.

I wiped my groggy eyes, and then it occurred to me that, yes, in fact, I do. I have insurance! I am insured in case something happened!

I silently thanked Dad for bullying me into responsibility, and told J.J., "Of course, I have insurance. I'm not a child!"

Contributed by: Reprinted with permission, from Melissa Evans, City Editor for the *Press-Telegram*, Sunday edition (12/21/14) A3. She has been involved with the newspaper industry for over 18 years.

Mother/Daughter Talk

I came home from work one day, to find my ten year-old daughter, Stephanie, very upset. Some of her friends were mad at her, and decided the best way to show their anger was to spread a rumor around the school that she was smoking. The problem was the rumor rang somewhat true—she confessed to having tried to smoke earlier in the year, with these same friends.

My mind raged. Who are these "friends"? How dare they encourage my child to smoke! How hypocritical of them to smoke with her, then turn it against her! Turn the whole school against her! Ruin her reputation! Where were their parents?

I looked at my child. She stood there on the other side of the dining room table, looking at me, and trembling. I thought I had taught her better. This choice to smoke was so obviously wrong! Why didn't she see that, and stand up to them? Wasn't she stronger than that? Wasn't she smarter than that?

I moved toward her—and she moved away. For some reason, she didn't trust me.

Then it hit me. This was my failure, not hers. After all, she was only ten years old! And now she was dealing with other ten year-olds seeking revenge in their own ten year-old way.

I walked over to the couch and sat down. Then I asked her if she would sit on my lap.

She ran to me. I took her in my arms and held her. "Mama, my life is *ruined!*" She buried her head into me, and cried.

Ruined? Really? I knew in that moment a lecture on the dangers of smoking, or seeking acceptance from her peers wasn't going to do it. She also didn't need to hear how awful her friends were, or how disappointed I was that she had smoked. What was done was done. Nothing I could do would change that. To her, her world was crumbling. To her, her life was ruined. A little dramatic, but crumbling and ruined, nevertheless.

I never felt so doubtful in my life. So when in doubt, don't lecture. Probe. Ask questions.

"Are you ruined?"

"It's everything! Everything is ruined! I'm a total screw up."

"Honey, you are not a screw up . . ."

"Mom! Even second graders were asking me it I smoked!"

Okay, forget commentary. Stick to questions. "So, what did you say to them?"

"I didn't know what to say!" she cried back. "Because I did! I smoked!"

"Well . . .do you smoke now?"

"NO!" Her answer came back angry that I would ask such a question.

"Then how about saying to them, 'No, I don't smoke', because you don't. You wouldn't be lying."

She sat more upright. Something I said finally made sense to her. I added, "You could give them an eye-roll, like that's the stupidest question you ever heard!"

She laughed a little.

"Your granddaddy always told me to give things three days. Then things will get better."

She tilted her head. "How?"

"You have to get through three days."

So we laid out a plan. Tell the truth. If someone asks you if you smoke, the answer is no, complete with an eye-roll. Lay low. Don't keep the drama going, by saying mean things about these three friends to others. After three days, if you have followed the first two, the rumor will be old news, and no one will care.

The plan was good. I thought we were done. But she just sat there. "Are you okay?" I asked.

She nodded. "Thanks, Mama."

I got up and started dinner, or I should say my own home-made version of fast food. Stephanie appeared in the kitchen. "Does God think I'm bad?"

For five seconds, I don't think I blinked. I think I stammered something like, "Of course not. We all make mistakes. . ."

"Mistakes, you don't see coming. I knew what I did was wrong."

Flawless reasoning from a ten year-old.

"But did I ruin my life? Does God think I'm a bad person?"

My heart broke. Her feelings about this incident, incited by friends, would pass. This was not so much about her reputation now, as her relationship with God. Her belief in herself.

I did a rerun on what she told me. She had said her life was ruined. She had said she was a total screw up. Is this really what she was getting at? That, in God's eye, she was bad? If so, another three-day plan in place wasn't going to be a band-aid enough for me to help my daughter.

It was then that I saw some twine in the cupboard. I took it out, and cut off a long string. I gave it to her, and asked her to stretch the strand of twine out between her hands. She did.

I asked her what color it was. She said, "White."

I told her that colors are symbolic of other things. That red can symbolize passion. That purple can signify royalty. I told her that white symbolized purity.

Then I asked her to look more closely at the strand of twine.

"Is it really all white?" She leaned into it, then said she could see little speckles of brown, here and there, woven all throughout the twine.

I told her to pretend that this strand of twine was her life stretched out before her. Every small brown speckle was where in her life, she had made some mistakes, and made a few bad choices. She silently nodded.

I asked her again what color the twine was. She still said, "White."

Still pure.

She cried.

We both did.

Twenty-two years later, on Mother's Day, Stephanie told me she still remembered that talk. And how, for a ten year-old, it had made all the difference in the world.

Contributed by: Elizabeth Call, art teacher at Horace Mann School (K-8) in Hollywoood, CA.

ENDNOTE

Life is a series of circumstances. Life is all about experiences. And some of those exciting and noteworthy events include unplanned Teachable Moments. Those moments of possibility, important happenings—surprising, motivating, reminding, or inspiring—can make a huge difference in our lives. Often, the *feelings* of such events last longer than the event itself. There are teachable moments out there for all of us. Be alert for those special moments, seize them, and run with them.

*The little things
and little moments
aren't little.*
—Jon Kabat-Zinn

*We do not remember days,
we remember moments.*
—Cesare Pavese

ACKNOWLEDGEMENTS

Although many people were asked to share their Teachable Moments, the following few took the time, effort, and energy to write about their experiences. To all, I offer my profound gratitude:

Don Barrett
Mary Beth Bastio
David Beakel
Richard Bonneau
Grady P. Brown
Elizabeth Call
Barbara Kaye Cooper
Marsha P. Reeder
Joshua Dulaney
Charles A. Filius
Bernard Fishman, D.D.S.
Lee Gale Gruen
Maggie L. Headrick

Devra Z. Hill, Ph.D.
Steven R. Kutcher
D.L. Laux
Jeanie MacDonald
Jay Matson
Wayne M. Meinberg
Leslie Miklosy
Patricia Bunin
Robert A.
Nagourney, M.D.
Theresa Schultz
Corrie Terry
Sally Thompson
Melinda Wells

An Invitation To Connect

I would love to hear your thoughts about this book. Your comments, your own Teachable Moment stories, and questions are most welcome. You can contact me via email or snail mail:

Dr. Sherry L. Meinberg
5417 E. Harco Street
Long Beach, CA 90808

sherrymeinberg@verizon.net